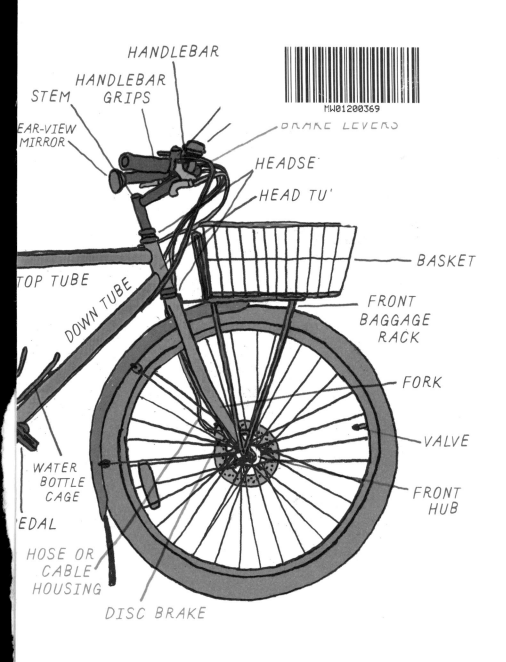

HANDLEBAR

HANDLEBAR
GRIPS

STEM

REAR-VIEW
MIRROR

BRAKE LEVERS

HEADSE'

HEAD TU'

BASKET

TOP TUBE

DOWN TUBE

FRONT
BAGGAGE
RACK

FORK

VALVE

WATER
BOTTLE
CAGE

FRONT
HUB

PEDAL

HOSE OR
CABLE
HOUSING

DISC BRAKE

BIKE LIFE

AN ILLUSTRATED GUIDE TO RIDING, FIXING, AND LOVING YOUR BIKE

Choosing
a Bike
p. 13

Riding
p. 67

Basic Settings
& Adjustments
p. 35

Mobility,
Health,
Savings, Joy,
Travel
p. 89

The Gear
That Goes
With You
p. 49

Maintenance &
Small Repairs
p. 105

The Components
of a Bike
p. 127

ADRIEN ZAMMIT

THE EXPERIMENT

NEW YORK

"Grab a bike,
free yourself!"
—Motto of the Vélorution,
an international movement to
liberate us from polluting and
dangerous vehicles

"The day I understood that I could easily
get from A to B if I followed my own rhythm
was the day this machine became a real way of
life. Biking is a wonderful moment of
introspection and personal advancement—and
one which is much cheaper than a shrink."
—Élise "Cabergnon" Sauvinet

"To build the desire for something you
need is to engage in the labor
of human happiness."
—Paul Fournel, *Need for the Bike*

This guide dreamed of being fully comprehensive and, of course, it isn't. The bike is simultaneously an object and an activity, and it brews countless insights! But with a bit of practice, some conversations with fellow cyclists, and diligent study of this weighty tome (☺), most human beings can feel relaxed and confident in the saddle.

I'm not going to talk about environmental issues in these pages. Everyone can manage to make the link between an ecosystem that is going down the drain and the individual and collective need to develop ways of living that are fairer, more generous, more economical. Let's go easy on the stern commands for individual eco-responsibility, and let's be realistic about the false promises of greenwashing, with its dashed-off cycle lanes and financial incentives to buy expensive and not especially durable bikes. Sorry, but riding a bike is not going to be enough to shoot down capitalism, its harshness, its industrial empires, and its Trojan horse: consumerism. After all, bicycles are themselves products.

Even so, getting out on a bike brings plenty of good things with it: You can cut your travel expenses (and perhaps work less as a result?); it's a quick and reliable means of making small door-to-door journeys; it keeps your body and your mind oxygenated and healthy; you support Main Street rather than lifeless strip malls and urban spread; you find yourself more connected to the people whose paths you cross along the way, and more in harmony with the land and its seasons. Finally, it's pure class when you arrive somewhere far from home via pedal power. The bike is a great tool to advance a more fulfilling and sensitive relationship with the living world.

May the wind be always at your back, my friends!

PARTS OF THE BIKE

A bike is made up of about 30 separate pieces. Gradually learning the role of each one, and how it works, makes this machine seem even more fabulous!

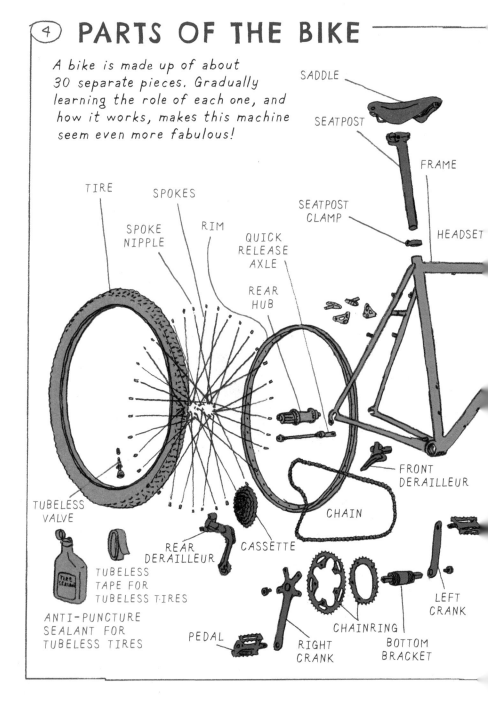

SADDLE

SEATPOST

FRAME

TIRE

SPOKES

SPOKE NIPPLE

RIM

SEATPOST CLAMP

HEADSET

QUICK RELEASE AXLE

REAR HUB

TUBELESS VALVE

REAR DERAILLEUR

CASSETTE

FRONT DERAILLEUR

CHAIN

TUBELESS TAPE FOR TUBELESS TIRES

ANTI-PUNCTURE SEALANT FOR TUBELESS TIRES

PEDAL

RIGHT CRANK

CHAINRING

LEFT CRANK

BOTTOM BRACKET

TIRE SEALANT

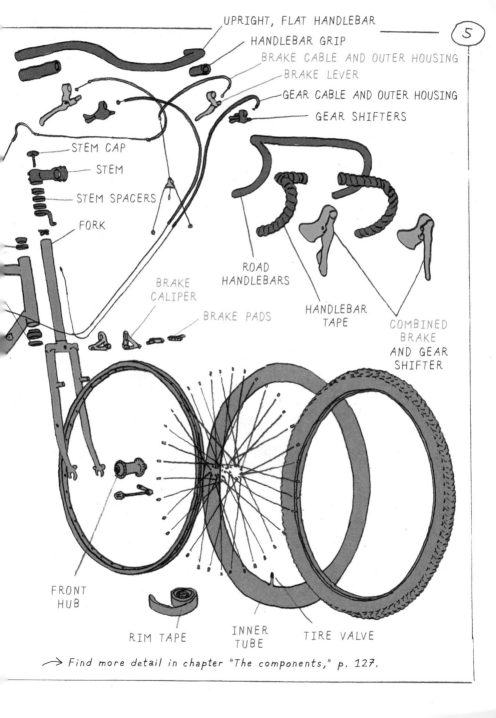

UPRIGHT, FLAT HANDLEBAR

HANDLEBAR GRIP

BRAKE CABLE AND OUTER HOUSING

BRAKE LEVER

GEAR CABLE AND OUTER HOUSING

GEAR SHIFTERS

STEM CAP

STEM

STEM SPACERS

FORK

ROAD
HANDLEBARS

BRAKE
CALIPER

BRAKE PADS

HANDLEBAR
TAPE

COMBINED
BRAKE
AND GEAR
SHIFTER

FRONT
HUB

RIM TAPE

INNER
TUBE

TIRE VALVE

→ Find more detail in chapter "The components," p. 127.

A SUPER-BRIEF

<u>1817</u>: Karl Drais von Sauerbronn invents the balance bike— "running machine" or "hobbyhorse"— with its wheels, saddle, handlebar, and footbrake. Still unparalleled for learning how to balance on two wheels.

<u>End of the 19th century:</u> A flood of inventions help the bicycle take form, notably the crankset (1861), the tire (1868), the chain (1879), the inner tube (1891), the freewheel (1894), and the derailleur (1895).

Women quickly take to the bicycle "I think it has done more to emancipate women than anything else in the world." —Susan B. Anthony, 1880

<u>Beginning of the 20th century:</u> With the arrival of mass production, the bike moves from a middle-class leisure activity to a popular method of transport. Prices fall quickly—in 1910, it took five weeks of work for a laborer to be able to afford a bike, but no more than a week and a half in 1930.

From a Western
European perspective

At the same time, cycling is becoming a media sport through popular competitions.

The Tour de France is launched in 1903 by L'Auto newspaper, founded three years earlier by an automobile industrialist of far-right political leanings to compete with the very popular Le Vélo. The aim of the "biggest cycling event ever organized" is to increase sales of L'Auto to sink its rival more effectively and to show that, incidentally, France is suitable for cars: If the proles can cross it by bike, then its beautiful landscapes are clearly within the reach of motorists!
A brilliant advertising stunt to sell cars to a still-skeptical middle class.

The '50s to today:
The development of the bike as a mode of transport is stymied by car-favoring policies such as the interstate highway system, suburban development, and more. It will take until the 2000s to see its return, amid the urgent need to reduce congestion in big towns and to cut CO_2 emissions. In urban settings, enthusiasm for cycling is reignited by the arrival of bike share schemes and, off the beaten track, by mountain bikes, bikepacking, and gravel riding.

WHAT MAGIC KEEPS YOU BALANCED ON A BIKE?

The gyroscopic effect is a force created by the movement of a disk that turns on its axis, allowing it to balance once it reaches a certain speed.

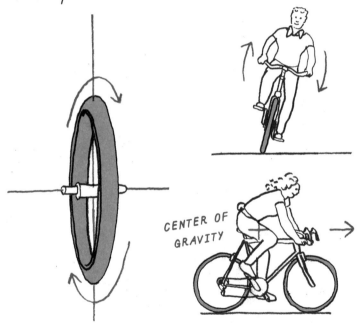

CENTER OF GRAVITY

By being placed laterally, the pedals create a counterbalance when you push down on them. On two moving wheels, balance is maintained thanks to successive alternating pedal strokes, steering, and the body's weight, which is supported mainly by the saddle.

HOW TO STOP

The rotating motion of the wheel can be slowed or
stopped by the brake and its clamping action on the
rim or disc. It is connected by a cable or hose to
a controller—a lever—which sits on the handlebar.

Using brakes → p.72

Brake lever on an upright, flat handlebar

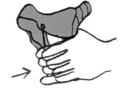

Brake lever on a road handlebar

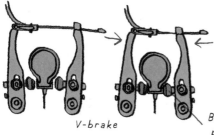

V-brake

Brake pads

Road brake

The rim brake is made up of a caliper with a pair of arms,
and brake pads which come into contact with the wheel to
slow it down. The rubber doesn't harm the surface of the
rims and provides reliable braking.

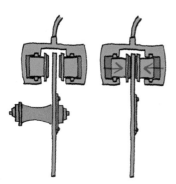

The disc brake comes from motorcycles
and cars. It consists of a caliper
that holds a pair of pistons and two
pads made out of resin or metal. The
pistons are activated by tension on
the cable (in the case of a mechanical
brake) or by the pressure of the
liquid contained in the hose
(hydraulic brake) so that the brake
pads firmly pinch the disc.

More details on brakes → p.136

HOW IS EFFORT TURNED INTO MOVEMENT?

Energy from your legs and the pedaling motion set off the rotation of the rear wheel. This mechanism is powered by the crankset in the center of the frame (pedals, cranks, and chainrings), driving a chain which in turn moves the cassette (collection of sprockets) on the rear wheel. The derailleurs are the guides. Drivetrain in detail → pp. 132–135

SPROCKETS
Serrated cogs (commonly called gears) which make up the cassette.

REAR DERAILLEUR

DERAILLEURS
These stop the chain from coming off and can move it to different cogs in order to change gears. The rear derailleur guides the chain on the sprockets, the front one on the chainrings. The movements are controlled by shift levers on the handlebar near to the brakes or, historically, on the top tube.
Certain bikes have only one derailleur (at the rear), or a gear system integrated into the rear hub, or even no derailleur at all (single speed or fixie).

FREEHUB BODY
If the rear wheel continues to move once you stop pedaling, thereby stopping the chain from turning, then it's thanks to a subtle mechanism of ratchets hidden in the body of the freehub—the part that is offset from the rear hub. The cassette is attached to it and only lets the wheel turn in the right direction.

CHAIN

Drive belt, consisting of
links that precisely glide
into the teeth on the
chainrings and sprockets.

FRONT DERAILLEUR

CHAINRINGS

Serrated cogs fixed
onto the pedal cranks

- p. 27 for details on
  how to choose the right
  drivetrain system
- p. 70 for details on
  how to change gears

The size of the chainring or
sprocket = its number of teeth

Gear ratio = $\dfrac{\text{size of chainring}}{\text{size of sprocket}}$

= the number of times the rear wheel
turns with one turn of the pedals

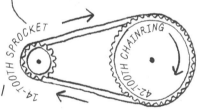

14-TOOTH SPROCKET

42-TOOTH CHAINRING

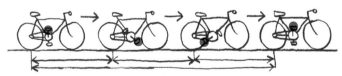

Gear development = the gear ratio x the circumference
of the wheel = the distance that the wheel travels with one
turn of the pedals. The smaller the wheel, the less distance
a gear ratio will cover.

CHOOSING A BIKE

OK, let's go! Even with a small budget, you can set yourself up nicely. But there's so much choice in stores or online...

What are the most important criteria for acquiring a bike that suits you? Aside from those relating to stylishness, of course. ☺

The bike as a means of transportation is not a luxury item. With around $150 to $300, you can find a nice secondhand machine for pleasant little journeys.

At $500 to $1,000, a reliable, comfortable bike well suited to daily trips.

The central thing is the frame!
You can make a number of adjustments and improvements to a bike but can't necessarily perform miracles: check out p. 24 on selecting the ideal size of bike, p. 27 the transmission type, pp. 28–29 for the type of wheels and the size of tires that will work.

> "Having a good bike changes everything. I can get up any climb and even if I slow down it's not the end of the world—I keep going and admire the countryside. It's great and doesn't cause me any hassle at all. My old bike wore me down after a while—for certain climbs in town I had to get off and push it."
> —Tatiana, costume designer and bike commuter

FAMILIES OF BIKES

MULTIPURPOSE BIKES

	Hybrid	Touring Bike	Gravel Bike	Touring Bike	'90s rig mountai bike
Position(s) p. 26	Comfortable	Sporty	Comfortable/ Sporty	Comfortable	Comfortal
Maneuverability	★★★★	★★★	★★★★	★★★★★ When luggage-free	★★★★★
Wheel diameter p. 28	700	700 or 650B	700 or 650B	26 inches 700 more rarely	26 inche
Potential for large tires (= comfort) p. 29	Meh	Not really	Yes	Meh	Yes, yes, ye
Gearing for heavy loads & big slopes p. 27	★★★	★★★	★★★★	★★★★★★★	★★★★★★★
Potential for luggage rack & mudguard	Often already installed	Already installed	Depends on the model	Already installed	Depend on the model
Suited to rough roads	★★★	★★	★★★★★	★★★★★	★★★★★
Suited to long distances	★★★	★★★★★	★★★★★	★★★★★★	★★★★★
Good for off-road (mud, stones, roots…)	No	No	★★★	★★★	★★★★★
Speed on the road	★★★	★★★★★	★★★★	★★★	★★★
Best price for a decent setup	$100– 500	$500– 1,000	$800– 1,500	$500– 1,200	$150 400

COMPARATIVE TABLE

UTILITY BIKES			FAST BIKES			LEISURE
City Bike	Cargo & long-tail	Folding	Road Bike	Recumbent	Fixie	Modern Mountain Bike
Upright	Upright/ comfortable	Upright	Sporty/ Racing	Comfortable	Sporty/ Racing	Comfortable/ Sporty
★★★ ★★	★★★	★★★★	★★	★	★	★★★ ★★
700 650B 26"	26" & 20" or 700 or other...	from 12" to 26"	700	Depends on the model	700	29" or 27.5"
Meh	Yes	Meh	Really not	Depends on the model	No	Yes, yes, yes
Depends on the model	★★★★★	★★★	No	Depends on the model	No	★★★★ ★★★
Already installed	Already installed	Often already installed	No	Depends on the model	No	No
No	No	No	No	Depends on the choice of tire	No	★★★
No	★★	No	★★★	★★★★★	★	★★
No	No	Absolutely not	No way	No, no, no	No go	★★★★★ ★★★
★★	★★★	★★	★★★★★ ★★★	★★★★★ ★★★	★★★★★ ★★★	★★
$50– 500	$500– 5,000	$150– 1,000	$300– 1,000	$500– 1,500	$200– 800	$800– 2,500

> **MY FAVORITES** Excellent steeds for 87.99% of humans!
> They are comfortable and dynamic for daily trips
> (even if these aren't their speciality…) and show
> their excellence as soon as routes become longer.

HYBRID

→ Leisure touring or "trekking" bike

Designed for quiet, fairly flat routes, the hybrid is pretty reliable and well suited to everyday use.

Big box stores sell this type of bike. To be avoided. (Like everything else you can find there!)

Ladies' versions are available, with a lowered top tube

Raised and curved "trekking" handlebars; very comfortable

Sturdy touring tires

Rigid or suspension fork
+ comfort, ← weight, and maintenance

RANDONNEURING/SPORT TOURING

A road bike focused more on comfort than performance.
A classic of the biking golden age of the '60s and '70s, designed and equipped for long days and long journeys in the saddle.

Leather saddle

Comfortable road handlebar, allowing multiple positions

Handy chrome pannier rack and mudguard

Front dynamo light

Few brands still have them among their line-ups

Road tires

GRAVEL BIKE

Go-anywhere adventure bike

A bike favoured by city dwellers who fancy being sporty, road riders who want comfort and to escape the asphalt, skilled mountain bikers tired of gimmicky gadgets, and cyclo-tourists when in "taking it easy" mode.

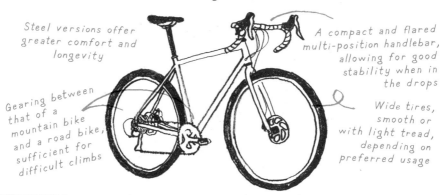

Steel versions offer greater comfort and longevity

A compact and flared multi-position handlebar, allowing for good stability when in the drops

Gearing between that of a mountain bike and a road bike, sufficient for difficult climbs

Wide tires, smooth or with light tread, depending on preferred usage

TOURING BIKE

Designed for embarking on big adventures—super well-equipped, stable, and robust. Rather heavy, but perfect for riding with peace of mind.

Reinforced steel frame

'90s RIGID MOUNTAIN BIKE

A type of recycling that I adore—getting hold of an old top-of-the-range steel mountain bike and then equipping it for urban riding.

Trekking handlebar → p. 45

Big, wide tires → p. 39

Bikes designed for small trips in towns or cities.
Practical, comfortable, and safe!

CITY BIKE

Well equipped—reassuring for beginners and for anyone who
is ill at ease in the saddle. Old- and Dutch-style models are
as elegant as they are heavy and are only suited to flat
roads.

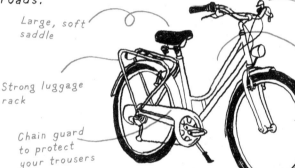

Large, soft
saddle

City-style
handlebar,
set high

Strong luggage
rack

Lowered
top tube to
make it easy
to mount

Chain guard
to protect
your trousers

Reinforced tires

SELF-SERVICE HIRE BIKE
(bike share schemes)

Very heavy (around 45 pounds) and sturdy, but the advantages
of town cycling mean that a ride on these machines is pleasant
nonetheless.

Many subscriptions are rather economical,
giving you access to unlimited no-charge
rides for the first 45 minutes.

Doesn't know how to
swim, but seems to
crave the water,
based on how many of
these can be found
resting at the bottoms
of urban waterways
everywhere.

CARGO AND LONGTAIL

It's not just in Asia or Africa that the bike is used to move heavy or bulky loads! A vehicle that is likely to become more and more common in urban settings as it supplements family or company cars.

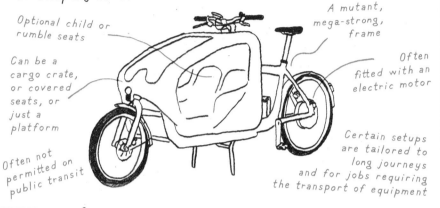

Optional child or rumble seats

A mutant, mega-strong, frame

Can be a cargo crate, or covered seats, or just a platform

Often fitted with an electric motor

Often not permitted on public transit

Certain setups are tailored to long journeys and for jobs requiring the transport of equipment

FOLDING BIKE

The ideal partner with which to combine methods of transport (mixed-mode commuting cocktails → p.96) and/or to have always with you—which is a good anti-theft technique. In a few steps, it's folded! With its small wheels, it's great fun to ride.

Adjustable seatpost for those of tall stature

A famous English brand has been making a model that is as reliable as it is compact since the '80s

There are electrically assisted versions of utility bikes, hybrids, mountain bikes, and road bikes—for two or three times the price, with similar quality components.

It's also possible to add an electric motor to a "normal" bike, presuming it has a suitable frame, brakes, and wheels. This is a reversible and relatively economical option.

The e-bike is noteworthy for each car that it manages to replace, and encourages more people to enjoy the benefits of cycling: low impact and silent, perfect for many door-to-door journeys, the pleasure of fresh air and of riding...

By the way, we mustn't forget the social and environmental problems linked to the batteries these bikes use (which have to be changed every two to five years with daily use), and the power plants that e-bikes and other electrical devices continue to keep in business. Motor-assisted riding is of clear interest for:

Regular journeys with heavy loads and/or across long distances

Life in areas that are far from flat

Those who have physical limitations

Could the assistance given by e-bikes also be seen as a step to getting (back) into cycling? Once you've got a taste of it, it seems difficult to live without it...

Remember: You still have to pedal for the electrical assistance to click in. Local laws vary: electric motors fitted on normal bikes are federally limited in the US to 28 mph—a speed that's quickly reached on flat ground with a decent bike and legs with a bit of training in them. When the motor cuts out, these machines become stupid heavy.

Helmet not compulsory in most states, no need for insurance or for a license.

ROAD BIKE

A light and responsive machine, designed for performance. You can easily get up speed and get over climbs without much training. A fragile and uncomfortable bike, it's to be reserved for seasoned or reckless riders.

No eyelets for a luggage rack.

Fragile wheels and tires.

Gearing that isn't well suited to the hardest climbs unless you've done some training.

"Compact"-style road handlebars are more ergonomic than the classic style. Also available with flat, "fitness"-style handlebars.

No space for mudguards or for comfortable tires.

RECUMBENT

A great position: aerodynamic and comfortable. Perfect for traveling with a wide view ahead of you, but not great for stopping and restarting or negotiating the zigzagging paths and traffic of a town.

There is a version with three wheels or with a mega-aerodynamic frame

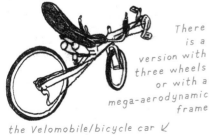

the Velomobile/bicycle car ↙

FIXED GEAR (FIXIE)

Originating in velodromes and gaining cult status among certain riders, the fixie has one gear and no free wheel: Your legs are permanently connected to the movement of the wheels, creating a heady dynamic for training.

Not to be confused with the single-speed, which has a freewheel

Used for bike polo

LEISURE BIKES

MOUNTAIN BIKE

Invented in the US in the late '70s, mountain biking has become a hugely successful pastime with, today, 10 subdisciplines connected to a large range of machines. Great toys for riding on trails but less good on roads or gravel.

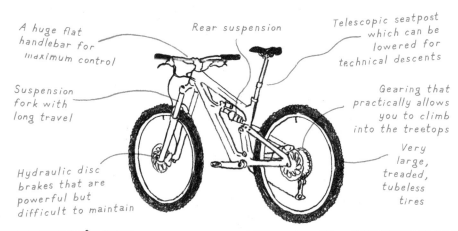

A huge flat handlebar for maximum control

Rear suspension

Telescopic seatpost which can be lowered for technical descents

Suspension fork with long travel

Gearing that practically allows you to climb into the treetops

Hydraulic disc brakes that are powerful but difficult to maintain

Very large, treaded, tubeless tires

TANDEM

The bike that attracts the most affection when out and about! Great for routes that don't have too many stops or twists and turns. Takes a bit of practice to be able to ride in synchronicity

In the rear seat you don't have to do much beyond pedaling if you fancy it, admiring your partner's muscles, and thoroughly enjoying the countryside as it passes by.

When on the front, you've got the responsibility of piloting the bike (steering, braking, gears) and a mental load that's doubled.

There are road versions, hybrid versions, touring versions...

Difficult if not against the rules to carry on most public transit.

BMX

A small daredevil bike that preceded the mountain bike, the BMX is used for races on circuits dedicated to it or for acrobatics in the air or around town.

Very low saddle, which you only rarely sit on while pedaling

TALL BIKE

A mutant machine often created in community bike shops, ideal for city and town festivals.

Assembled from salvaged frames

QUADRICYCLE/ PEDAL GO KART

Barely more practical than rail-bikes (tandems or four-seater bikes that are equipped to ride along rail lines), but long live collective efforts at movement without a motor!

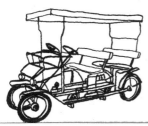

BIKES ADAPTED FOR THOSE WITH DISABILITIES

• **The recumbent tricycle,** with its seat and multiple possible configurations
• **The handcycle,** with its hand crank
• *Tandems*

The best way to get a sense of the different sizes, frame types, and riding positions is to <u>test ride several bikes</u> that match your criteria and your body type,* spending at least 30 minutes on each—and maybe even as much as a day. You can borrow friends' bikes or test models available in stores!

*Bike brands have their own tables to help you work out which size would suit you best, which are a good place to start. Worth bearing in mind that a small in one brand doesn't necessarily correspond to a small in another. ☺

Frame that's too big and/or handlebar stem that's too long

→ A position that's too stretched out!

Arms and back at around 90 degrees is a good position for long rides

Saddle and handlebar at about the same level

Frame too small → position too slumped!

A frame that's (a little) too big can actually be really good if it's fitted with a handlebar stem that is high and short, and a relaxed handlebar or one that slopes backward.

A frame that is (a little) too small is only suited to those who are passionate about performance and in search of an edge.

*If you have trouble figuring out the adjustments needed to make a bike and position fit for you (→ pp. 40–45), you could always treat yourself to a professional fitting at a bike store.

THAT FITS

AND FOR THOSE OF SMALLER STATURES?

Pay attention to the height of the top tube. If it touches your groin when you're stopped (with two feet on the ground), then it's no good. Possible solutions to this problem are:
• A sloping frame geometry (with a slanted top tube)
• Low crank arms (≠ mountain bike or fixie)
• 27.5 inch/650B or 26-inch wheels rather than 700 (→ p.28)

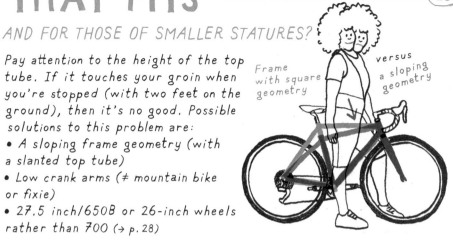

Frame with square geometry   versus a sloping geometry

Toe overlap is when you're pedaling at a gentle speed and the tip of your foot comes into contact with the front wheel. Common with a small frame + big wheel + mudguard combination... It's a bit weird, but you get used to it. Not dangerous, unless you're riding barefoot!

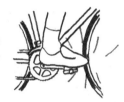

AND FOR THE LADIES?

"Ladies" versus "male" geometry—nuanced differences of a few inches, but ones that count!

No matter your gender, if you have longer legs and a shorter torso than the "norm"* then you need a fairly compact and high frame with a short handlebar stem. That said, frame geometries aren't really standardized and vary between models.** The width of the handlebars also needs to be taken into account, linked to the width of your shoulders.
*Shall we talk about the patriarchy of objects?
**See bikeinsights.com to compare geometries

A "mixed" frame geometry (commonly referred to as "ladies'") makes it easy to get on and off the bike, especially if you're wearing a skirt or if you're not especially flexible. In general these frames lack a bit of rigidity, which isn't ideal for efficiency or for transporting heavy loads.

POSITION

You're looking for comfort, a feeling of dynamism and energy, and a good distribution of weight, rested mainly on your butt and a little on your hands. The upper body is simultaneously relaxed and engaged in effort.

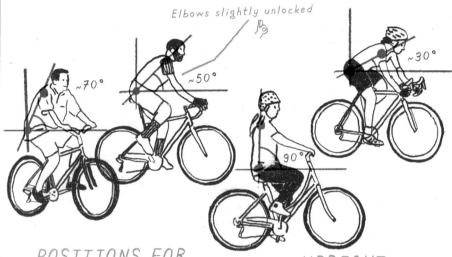

Elbows slightly unlocked

~70° ~50° 90° ~30°

POSITIONS FOR COMFORT/SPORT

Saddle and handlebar at about the same height, back sloped between 50 and 75 degrees. Perfect for pretty much everyone, regardless of the length of journey and the flexibility of the rider.

UPRIGHT

Back straight (90 degrees), really only pleasant for short journeys. No weight on the arms → the back and the buttocks absorb all the bumps in the road, which is tiring and perhaps even painful, plus bad transmission of effort and heavy wind resistance.

RACING POSITIONS

Virtually lying flat, depending on how you ride and your physiology; ideal when facing the wind but requires training (and yet more training!) to pull off, tiring for the arms, neck, and back. Not great in town settings— nose on the handlebar and butt among the cars!

When testing a position, you need to make sure to adjust the height of the saddle first (→ p. 40).

GOOD GEARING

Or: how to have enough "gears" to suit your riding?

What the heck are gears and gear ratios? → p.13

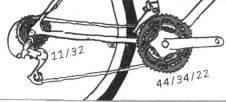

11/32

44/34/22

Hybrid- or '90s mountain bike-style transmission

11/46

40

One chainring gravel-style transmission Smallest gear ratio = 40/46 = 0.9

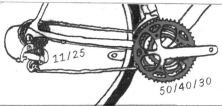

11/25

50/40/30

Road touring—style transmission Smallest gear ratio = 30/25 = 1.2

11/28

50/36

Compact, road-style transmission Smallest gear ratio = 36/28 = 1.3

To cope with difficult climbs while carrying a load and on the road, a smallest gear ratio of about 0.8 works well; 0.7 or 0.6 are even better! For example: 38 small chainring / 46 largest sprocket; 34/40; 30/36 And if that's not enough, then frankly you wouldn't be going all that much slower if you got off and pushed! The smaller the wheels, the farther you'll go in the same gear.

8, 9, or 10 well-spaced gears are enough for leisure riding on any surface. Careful: The number of gears on a bike doesn't indicate the difference in ratio between the biggest gear and the smallest, nor that the latter will be enough in the hardest parts of a route.

Example: with a 3 chainrings / 10 sprockets (30 gears) drivetrain, several gears overlap and around six are unusable because they would make the chain cross (→ p. 71). Modern drivetrains with lots of gears are for cyclists who are looking to optimize their performance on a bike, or who are just pedants.

For a light touring bike to be used on road and gravel, I recommend a single chainring with 38 or 40 teeth and an 11/46 cassette with 9, 10, or 11 sprockets. Drivetrains with two or three chainrings don't wear out the chain as quickly, but are less smooth to use, more laborious to install and to maintain, and carry a greater risk of the chain slipping off or breaking.

WHEEL SIZE

Design of frame and forks
= possible diameters for wheels
= a maximum possible tire width

DIAMETERS

The bigger the wheel, the easier it is to get it rolling after a stop and the greater the inertia—so it is more efficient. The smaller the wheel, the greater its stability and handling.

The diameter in millimeters mentioned below is that of the wheel rim. The width (and so the height) of the tire when inflated plays into the total diameter.

The three current diameters:

700C

ETRTO 622 mm (European Tyre and Rim Technical Organisation), 28 inches for tires up to 48 mm, 29 inches for tires of 2-inch width or more (mountain bike)

Traditional diameter for rims on road bikes and more recently used for mountain bikes as it helps with the ability to clear obstacles. To put it simply, the fastest option available.

27.5 INCH

ETRTO 584 mm (also known as "650B")

A very good compromise between a comfortable and zippy ride. Good choice if you want a bike that goes anywhere, and for people of smaller stature.

26 INCH

ETRTO 559 mm

The standard for hybrids and mountain bikes up until the middle of the aughts. Still found on touring bikes, small frames, and on cheap bikes. Very good for urban riding and for trails.

Measurements for components are given in mm or cm, except for pieces from American brands (gear for mountain bikes) which are measured in inches. 1 inch = 25.4 mm.

Air costs nothing in weight or cash, but has great value for enjoyment while riding!

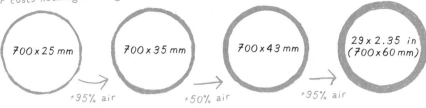

700 x 25 mm → +95% air → 700 x 35 mm → +50% air → 700 x 43 mm → +95% air → 29 x 2.35 in (700 x 60 mm)

The quality and volume of its tires can transform how a bike rides.

To offer the most potential for this transformation, it's best to choose a bike with a frame and fork that can accommodate wide tires.

Assuming tires of equal quality and the right air pressure (p.38), the size and volume of a tire will have very little impact on speed but an enormous impact on comfort!

"The narrower the tire, the faster it goes" is a myth that comes from competitive cycling, where the slightest ounce and aerodynamic improvement counts for shaving a few precious seconds off times. Narrow tires have to be inflated to a high pressure,* which makes bikes uncomfortable, more unsafe, and more energy-sapping. Imperfections in road surface are barely absorbed, which slows the bike and means lots of vibrations reverberating in the body.

*Tire pressure recommendations p. 38

OPTIMAL SIZES → p. 39 for advice on "good tires" and p. 114 for advice on how to change them

- For a comfortable road bike: 700 x 32 to 38 mm
- For a go-anywhere bike (roads and gravel): 700 x 38 to 45 mm or 27.5 inches (650B) x 42 to 50 mm or 26 inches x 2.15 to 2.35 inches
- For a trail mountain bike: 29 inches x 2 to 2.30 inches or 27.5 inches x 2.2 to 2.50 inches

Things to pay attention to when assessing the state of a bike and to set off in complete confidence!

Keep them in mind for regular checks of the state of your bike.

FRAME AND FORK

☞ Nothing dented, no breaks nor any rust (for steel components)?

☞ No twists in the fork?

☞ Seatpost and stem not welded to the frame (if steel)?

Metals bend or crack before breaking. Steel frames are more durable than aluminum, so long as you pay attention to any corrosion, and are the only "easy" metal frames to repair—if the problem is repairable at all, that is. Buying a secondhand carbon (= plastic) bike is a risk, because any erosion of fibers isn't detectable to the naked eye… and, one day, it'll break.

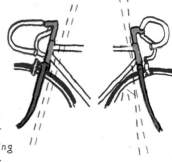

WHEELS

☞ No buckling of the rims, no bumps or cracks?

Move sideways

☞ Rim brakes: No grooves or curving in the rim's braking surface.

☞ Consistent spoke tension (test by pinching them in pairs).

☞ Hubs: No lateral movement of the wheel, and bearings move smoothly.

☞ Axle: Check that the wheels are well centered and safely attached.

Quick release axle: Undo the lever and then close it again. If it feels too loose, tighten the nut a little.

Open, twist, close

- _Tires:_ Check pressure by pushing down on the wheel with your full weight or by pinching the tire. It should not seem soft. How's it look? Is the tread badly worn down? Are the sides cracked or worn...? A tire that's on its last legs must be replaced so as to avoid repeated punctures and to stay safe (p. 114).

Brake and push

BRAKES AND SHIFTING

- Brakes not powerful enough? Adjust them as needed (p. 36).

- It's tricky to accurately judge braking and shifting with just a glance and with a quick test...

  There are several parts that can wear out and that can be to blame for malfunction, requiring either adjustment (p. 118) or replacement: chain (p. 116), brake pads (p. 115), cables and cable housing, bottom bracket, cassette and chainring, derailleur cages...

Brake and push

Secure the front wheel and try to turn the handlebars

- Tightly secured and no play in the pedals, cranks, headset, handlebar?

  <u>Take it for a little ride and keep an ear out for the slightest creak, the tiniest weird grinding sound...</u>

You could always check out the classifieds. Sending a bike in the mail needn't cost a fortune, but requires a fair bit of dismantling and packing work! Take the time to speak to the seller on the phone, to ask for photos, to check how the owner's size compares to your own, to ask why they're selling, about any parts that will need changing, whether that's their best price, etc.

FRAGILE

If you can't face the hassle—have neither time nor buddies to advise you and to help you grab a good deal—but do have moolah, then you opt for new!

A specialist bike store will undoubtedly find a good bike for you, whether from its existing stock or by placing an order, will help adjust and adapt the bike to your needs by changing a few parts, and will be there to help with any potential technical problems. Some even offer formal bike fitting.

It may be tempting to buy a new bike at a big-box store (especially the one that rhymes with "mall-cart"), but these bikes, while often extremely affordable, are cheaply made and often quickly end up in the landfill.

There are tons of _websites_ selling bike stuff. You can find complete bikes online, can land yourself a great bargain or a pile of crap. The search will be time-consuming, and you'll have to be ready to roll up your sleeves when the parcel arrives at your house.

What a joy to ride a bike on which each and every component was carefully selected by you, through an understanding of how the part will work and what benefits it will bring you!

WITH A PRO

Before launching into such a project, it's best to have a lot of cycling experience and to have test ridden several bikes to determine your exact requirements.

Certain bike stores and framebuilders can create a bespoke bike from one of their frames. It's a little more expensive, but to have something tailor-made is so lovely. You can even treat yourself to a personalized paint job, perhaps even with glitter (or not...)!

DO IT YOURSELF

Putting together a bike yourself is doable, but it takes time, specialist tools (p. 122), and an eye for detail. Why not join a cooperative bike shop (p. 124)? You can get hold of secondhand components, but it's generally a good idea to go new for cables, chain, and cassette.

BASIC SETTINGS & ADJUSTMENTS

Cycling should never be associated with pain! The competitive spirit, with its traumatic efforts and its bikes that are as light as they are fragile and uncomfortable, can be left in the locker room.

A well-adjusted riding position, a safe bike, and gradual improvement are the basis of pleasure.

The saddle, tires, and the front end of the bike all play a pretty big part in all that. They can be tweaked or changed as needed.

Desperate to get riding? At the very least, check the brakes, tire pressure, and make sure that everything you're carrying is safely secured (bike locks, baggage, etc.). And every so often, take the time to carry out a more thorough check of your bike (p. 30).

> "The advice I always give to my buddies: Adjust your saddle properly! It changes everything in terms of pressure on your groin."
> —Claire, bike commuter and traveler

ADJUST THE

COMMON CAUSES OF POOR BRAKING PERFORMANCE —

A BRAKE THAT'S TOO SOFT OR JUST TOTALLY USELESS

Most often linked to wear and tear of the brake pads (p. 115) and/or a cable which has slightly stretched over time.

• Mechanical brake: <u>Cable no longer tight enough?</u>
→ Tighten it by turning the barrel adjuster counterclockwise.
If this doesn't make enough of a difference, loosen the cable's connection to the brake caliper and then pull the cable slightly to tighten it by hand.

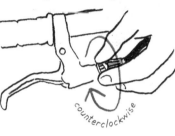

counterclockwise

If on the other hand a brake is <u>too sensitive</u> or its lever doesn't spring back easil it's likely the cable—and possib also the cable housing—that need changing!

• <u>Brake pads or discs too worn, or too "contaminated" with dirt?</u>
→ Change them.

Worn! Almost no more rubber left sticking out.

New

• Hydraulic brake: <u>Air bubbles in the hose?</u>
→ It needs bleeding (which in turn needs a bleed kit and some skill).

A BRAKE THAT'S RUBBING

• <u>Wheel seated badly?</u> → Open the axle and carefully reseat the wheel in the dropouts, all while the bike is resting on the ground on both its wheels

• Mechanical brake: <u>Cable too tight?</u>
→ Loosen it by turning the barrel adjuster clockwise. (See example above.)

BRAKES

A BRAKE THAT'S RUBBING (CONTINUED)

• Warped rim or disc?
→ Straighten (true) or replace!

• Brake rubbing on the rim:
Badly placed pads?
→ Have another look at their positioning
(both their height and the angle at
which they meet the wheel).

> The front of the
> brake pad needs
> to be slightly
> closer to the rim
> (about 0.5 mm
> more) to prevent
> it from squeaking.

• Off-center brake?
→ Adjust the two arms so that
the brake is re-centered.

V- or cantilever brake → Tighten/
loosen the small adjustment screws on
the sides of the caliper.
Road brake → Adjust by hand

Mechanical disc brake
→ Use the adjuster/s on the brake calipers.

Hydraulic disc brake
→ Loosen the frame mounting screws a little
to give a bit of play, then apply the brake so
that the caliper and pistons are realigned in
relation to the disc. While keeping the brake
on, retighten the frame mounting screws.

• Hydraulic brake: Pistons out
too far? → Take the wheel off and
push the brake pads back using a
clean flat screwdriver or
dedicated tool.

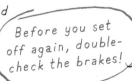

Before you set
off again, double-
check the brakes!

GOOD PRESSURE

The ideal tire pressure depends on the width of the tires, on the total weight (cyclist + bike + load), but also on the level of comfort the rider is seeking and the terrain being ridden. A foot pump with a pressure gauge is needed.

Tire pressure can easily drop, particularly in cold weather, so it should be regularly checked!

Tire pressure recommendation table inspired by Frank Berto's in *Bicycle Quarterly*

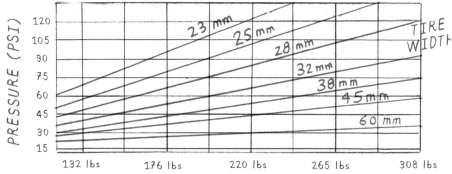

PRESSURE (PSI): 120, 105, 90, 75, 60, 45, 30, 15

23 mm, 25 mm, 28 mm, 32 mm, 38 mm, 45 mm, 60 mm — TIRE WIDTH

TOTAL WEIGHT OF THE CYCLIST + BIKE + BAGGAGE: 132 lbs, 176 lbs, 220 lbs, 265 lbs, 308 lbs

UNDERINFLATED TIRE

• Risk of puncturing the inner tube (when it becomes pinched between the rim and an obstacle) and of hitting the wheel rim (ouch!), especially if you're riding on narrow tires.

• Poor traction when cornering: DANGER!

• Sides of the tires (sidewalls) wear out more quickly.

OVERINFLATED TIRE

• Uncomfortable—the vibrations from defects in the road are poorly absorbed.

  • On trails: difficult to ride. You're thrown about all over the place, which is exhausting and dangerous. That's the main attraction of tubeless: You can ride at a low pressure.

How do you in/deflate your tire? → p. 10

THE RIGHT TIRES —

THE PERFECT TIRE IS A BALANCE BETWEEN RESISTANCE TO PUNCTURES, FLEXIBILITY, AND A GENEROUS VOLUME!

<u>The wider the tire</u> (p. 29), the greater the volume of air it contains and the more comfortable (cushioned) and safe it is (I'm soft)! Wide tires are soooooooo cool!

<u>The more flexible the tire</u> (well, the tire casing), the better vibrations are absorbed— which provides comfort, dynamism, and speed. The higher the tire's TPI (threads per inch), the lighter, more flexible, and more hard-wearing the tire. With two tires of the same width, the lighter of the two will generally be more supple but less durable. The quality of the rubber used for a tire does also greatly play into its properties.

Black tire sidewalls have a coating which protects against UV damage and against friction, unlike tan sidewalls (skin-walls).

<u>The thicker and more reinforced the tire, the stiffer and more ungainly the bike feels.</u> "Puncture-proof" tires should be reserved for chaotic towns or for very long journeys.

Anti-puncture layer

When used on smooth roads, knobby tires drag, wear more quickly, and don't grip particularly well in corners. They should be reserved for off-road use (gravel, mud, snow...)

→<u>TUBELESS TIRES?!</u> Tubeless tires are mounted on a special rim, with a dose of anti-puncture tubeless sealant replacing the inner tube (p. 114). If the tire is mounted properly, then you no longer have to worry about pinch punctures or small tears (from thorns and so on), because the liquid can plug those holes. To repair large punctures, you'll need a plug tool and a patch and/or an inner tube. Tubeless tires are a bit fiddly (it's not always easy to fit them), but they are great for being able to confidently ride on trails and offer a real bonus in comfort.

ADJUSTING

Correct adjustment does more for the comfort of a saddle than the choice of the saddle itself!

~170°

Your leg must not be straight when the pedal is at its lowest point. If you're having to extend your foot or your hips rock when you pedal, it's really not good!

Conversely, setting the saddle too low in search of greater "comfort" can cause knee injuries. That said, it's OK for short journeys or while you're building up your riding confidence.

① SADDLE HEIGHT

= the distance between the bottom bracket spindle and the top of the saddle.

→ **Setting while on the bike:**
When the crank is in its downward position—in line with the seatpost—and the back of your heel is in line with the back of the pedal, while the pedal is level, your leg should be more or less straight.

→ **Theory-based adjustment:**
Measure your inside leg in inches and multiply it by 0.88 to get your saddle height.

The appropriate height for a saddle also depends on the length of the cranks, the thickness of the soles on the shoes you'll be wearing… in short, it's not an exact science.

Inside leg in inches x 0.88

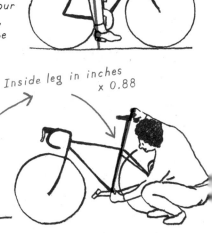

THE SADDLE

② FORE-AFT POSITION

<u>Traditional rule for adjusting:</u> When the pedals are both an equal distance from the ground, your knee should be in line with the front of the pedal.
<u>Another setting which works:</u> Put the saddle as far back as it will go.

It may be necessary to get a seatpost which allows the saddle to go back farther.

If you feel the need to move the saddle closer or to raise the handlebar, then you need to tweak the front end of your bike.

③ SADDLE ANGLE

We start by setting the saddle to an <u>angle of 0°</u>, parallel to the ground, and testing it at that setting.

→ People with a vulva can perhaps very slightly tilt the front of the saddle down to reduce pressure on the soft tissues of the perineum. This does however increase pressure on the arms and wrists, and leads to more tension in the cervical and trapezius muscles.

↘ If you've got pain in your wrists or the upper back, you can try very slightly tilting the saddle backward.

Once everything is properly set up, you should make only micro-adjustments to address any discomfort you feel on the bike (→ p.46). Once you are sure of the right height for your saddle, mark a line on the seatpost.

CHOOSING

The shape of a saddle is more important than what it's made from. This choice is a very personal one and depends largely on the space between your sit (ischial) bones (which form the bottom part of your pelvis). These bones have to support your body's weight when you are seated. The space varies depending on your body type and your position on the bike.

In an "aggressive" riding position (crouched), your weight will press on the pubic side.

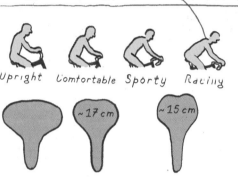

Upright   Comfortable   Sporty   Racing

~17 cm   ~15 cm

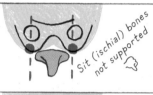

Sit (ischial) bones not supported

Sit (ischial) bones well positioned

ORDINARY SADDLES

Lightweight, inexpensive, not all that attractive to thieves. There are so many that every butt can find one that suits it. Extremely lightweight, top-of-the-range saddles have very little padding and so require cycling shorts. ☺

Plastic or leather covering with light padding underneath

Versatile, semi-rounded shape

SOFT SADDLES

"Comfortable"... for short trips only! It's a marketing ploy, because the softer a saddle the more your sit bones sink into it and so are unable to properly support your body. Tha means your groin has to support more weight and more friction.

Copious gel padding

Too wide for most rears = extra friction!

A SADDLE

LEATHER SADDLES

Leather +/- thick depending on brand = +/- breaking-in time and lifespan

Attractive, heavy, expensive, not vegan, don't like the rain, or the sun, or sweaty butts.

Renowned as being the best saddle for cyclo-touring: With use, the leather molds to your crotch and softens just enough. Has to be reshaped and "nourished" after a while.

Easy with greasing! It's useless when the saddle is new, and then should only be done once a year at most—the leather ages prematurely otherwise.

LADIES' MODELS

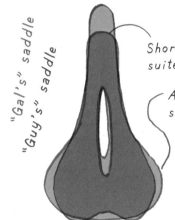

"Gal's" saddle

"Guy's" saddle

Short and/or soft saddle tip, suited to a lower pubic bone

Also practical when wearing a dress, skirt, or harem pants

A larger back of the saddle, suited to larger pelvises

For very sporty riders:
→ Women's cycling shorts or underwear → p.62

And for sporty riders of all genders:
→ A narrower saddle gives ample room to pedal and avoid chafing.

CUTOUT SADDLE

May be useful if you have perineal pain or other problems (fungal infections such as thrush, for instance). On the other hand, having a hollowed out (cutout) saddle can lead to greater stress on other areas of the body which may then cause pain.

If this happens, tweak your position as a priority (pp. 40 and 44).

No rear mudguard? You can put a cover on the saddle to avoid anything unpleasant flying through the cutout gap within it.

Having chosen a frame geometry and adjusted the saddle, the next thing that plays a role in your position on the bike is the stem and handlebars. Both can be changed.

It's best to choose a handlebar that's part of the same family as the original, whether flat/upright or road, because that means you don't have to replace any components that are fixed to it. → *Take this into account when choosing a bike!*

A multiposition handlebar (road or "butterfly" handlebars) is unbeatable for long journeys because it allows you to vary the position of your wrists, arms, and back, sparing you a lot of pain!

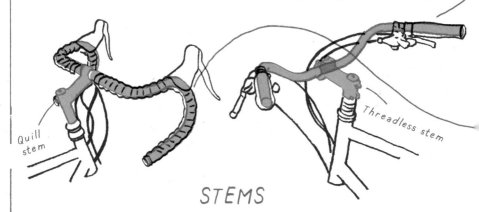

Quill stem

Threadless stem

STEMS

Available in everything from 30 mm to 150 mm and with a range of angles, from 0° to +/− 60°!

Pay attention to its compatibility with the fork and the handlebar.

- <u>Threadless stems</u> are attached to the steerer tube with a top cap, while <u>quill models</u> insert into the steerer tube with an extender. → p.129
- *Stems are measured by the diameter of the <u>steer tube they fit</u>: ∅ 1 in, 1.125 in...*
- *And finally stems for ∅ 25.4, 26, 31.8 mm diameter handlebars... Adjustable stems are adjustable in tilt only—they are heavy, ugly, and most become loose. They are really only useful while trying to find your ideal angle.*

FLAT (UPRIGHT) HANDLEBARS

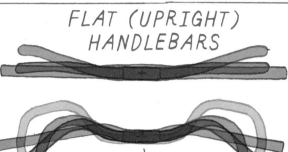

⌀25.4 or 31.8 mm

Some examples among the huge range of models:

Town bike cruiser-style handlebars—raised and wide; very comfortable

Trekking handlebars, notably wide and raised—nice for treks

Large and flat mountain biking handlebar, ideal for technical riding

Multiposition "butterfly" handlebars—simultaneously ugly and ergonomic

ROAD HANDLEBARS (DROPS)

These don't necessarily dictate a "crouched" position. When mounted on a frame and a stem adapted to your size, they are really nice. Varying designs are available (width, reach, drop, curve). Gravel and compact models are most suited to beginners and having fun.

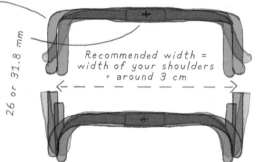

26 or 31.8 mm

Recommended width = width of your shoulders + around 3 cm

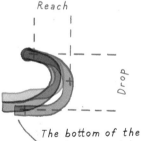

Reach

Drop

The bottom of the drops must be parallel to the ground

Classic, not-really-ergonomic, road handlebar
Compact road handlebar neither deep nor very high
Very compact gravel handlebar and flared at the bottom

Riding in the drops is aerodynamic—which means that, once you go above 12 mph, you economize on effort yet gain a bit of extra speed.

Riding in the drops with a gravel handlebar—body low and hands spaced far apart—gives increased stability and greater precision when the riding is technical.

OUCH, OUCH, OUCH?!

While riding, the body's weight rests on the sit (ischial) bones, the groin, and the wrists. The knees and Achilles tendons carry little weight but perform very repetitive movements, while the back, shoulders, and arms are called on a great deal to hold the body in place. Any pain has one of two causes: a poorly set up bike, or shortcomings in the muscles (strength, endurance, flexibility in the posterior muscles).

Whatever sort of pain you experience, keep an eye on how it progresses as you start riding regularly (while not overdoing it). Aches that appear after your first few bike rides are just linked to a lack of practice.

Practicing other sports or exercise alongside regular riding is highly recommended—it helps build your muscles and your flexibility.

Pain in the lower back: Position not straight enough? Too upright? Back too arched or abdominal muscles too relaxed? Paraspinal muscles need strengthening? Riding too hard?

Anal pain: Saddle tilted too far downward?

Pain in the soft tissues in the groin: Saddle too soft or too narrow? Riding for too long, or without enough breaks? Position too upright? Saddle too high? Need padded shorts or underwear or a cutout saddle?

Pain in the vulva or testicles: Saddle that's tipped too far upward? Position too crouched? Saddle too high? Front of saddle too hard?

Pain in the shoulders or neck: Handlebar too distanced (too low or too pushed forward) or too close (too high or too tipped back)? Shoulders and back muscles not quite strong enough yet?

Pain in the wrists or arms: Saddle tipped downward? Position too upright? Too stretched? Need a multiposition handlebar? Handlebar grips, tape, or cycling gloves not comfortable enough?

Pain in the hands: Poor positioning of the brake levers or bad handlebar angle? Insufficient handlebar width? Position that's not far enough forward? Over-padded gloves or handlebar tape?

Carpal tunnel pain: Bad back posture? Back extensors need strengthening? Gloves or handlebar tape too padded?

Swelling in the front of the knee: Saddle too low or too far forward? Pedaling too hard? Cranks too long?

Swollen joints: Poorly hydrated? Buttocks and thighs not quite muscular enough?

Swollen Achilles tendon or backs of the knees: Saddle too high?

Pain in the arch of the foot: Shoe soles too soft or too hard (high end models)? Cadence too low? Saddle tilted too far forward?

THE GEAR THAT GOES WITH YOU

A safe, peaceful, and comfortable ride doesn't just come down to the bike. You'll also need to spend a few extra bucks on accessories.

You need something to keep your bike secure, to make sure you can be easily seen (especially in the dark), to carry items or young passengers, to make repairs whether on the road or at home, to protect you from bad weather, and from the (very small) possibility of a nasty crash.

"When you don't have any other transportation options—when cycling has become your main or even your only transport method—all of its potential inconveniences are no longer there. Cycling became fully part of my life when our car gave up on us and we chose to neither repair nor replace it. Now when the morning rolls around I don't ask myself whether or not I'm going to take my bike, if it's perhaps too cold to ride, or if there's too much of a chance it'll rain, or if I have too many separate trips to make. It doesn't matter. I take my bike, with my rain jacket and my waterproof trousers in the bottom of my pannier, and off I go!"

—Pascaline, enthusiastic rider from the rainy north of France

LOCKS

There is no lock that will last long against a cordless electric bolt cutter but few bandits cart one of those around with them. A good quality* U-lock that can be attached to the wheels is the best protection if you need to leave your bike outdoors. Lock the bike to something solid and well anchored into the ground, and in a busy place.

*Sold Secure's respected rating system is a good reference.

And—so that it's no dented when you come back to it—make sure there is n chance its wheels are exposed to the possibility o being knocked by any vehicle that might be maneuverin nearby (a car that's parking, for example)

The U!

Mini U-locks are easy to carry around and impossible to lever off—unlike larger U-locks, which are known to be breakable with prying.

Old shortened chain or basic lock to secure the saddle to the frame(assuming the saddle is
precious).

This little lock can be enough for securing your bike when cyclo-touring during short stops, or while camping

Anti-theft axles, cable locks, or frame locks

A mini-U lock only allows you to attach the frame to something. With a classic U-lock, you can lock the frame to one of the wheels.

A second U-lock or a long chain for when leaving your bike overnight, for several days in a row, or in the same place regularly—even if that's the hallway of your building.

Around 30% of thefts are from enclosed spaces. This U-lock can be left attached to the stand at which you park your bike, in the same way motorcyclists leave their locks behind when they are out riding.

If you turn you bike upside down, you'll likely find a serial number engraved into the frame, on the underside of the bottom bracket. Many municipalities allow you to register this unique code, which can help reconnect you with your bike if it does get stolen.

Under homeowners or renters insurance, you can claim for the theft of a bike.

Forgot to bring locks and security devices with you? Then you find a way to keep your bike with you at all times—even if that means climbing up eight flights carrying it on your shoulder. It's times like these that you particularly enjoy having a lightweight bike.

LIGHTING
& REFLECTORS

Very important—and, unless you plan on being some sort of kamikaze ninja, mandatory at night or when traveling through tunnels.

Having a suitable lighting system is crucial to you being seen by other road users, and to you being able to see in areas where there is no street lighting.

IN WELL-LIT AREAS

Little lights running on rechargeable batteries.

Use on a low setting that gives constant light rather than one that is bright and flashes—it's less likely to blind others that way, and so safer for everyone.

Reflectors:

Cycling clothing with reflective elements

Reflectors (mandatory)

Tires with a reflective band on the sidewalls.

Reflective tape

At night, good reflectors will make you more visible to drivers than a small rear bike lamp will.

IN NON-LIT AREAS

A headlamp!

To be able to see to your sides, to help you see if you need to make a repair, to come to the rescue if your front light stops working... Certain models are specifically designed to be worn with a bike helmet. The flashlight on your phone should be your last resort—it's not practical.

A yellow reflective vest HEY! HEY!

Vital when riding at night outside of well-lit areas.

A light that shines well without dazzling people passing in the other direction. Halogen or LED, either battery- or dynamo-powered.

Modern dynamos are integrated into the front hub. This is efficient and—depending on the price of the model you choose—not particularly heavy.

If you are only occasionally riding at night in non-lit areas, then you may not need a powerful front lamp—a small front light might be enough.

HELMET

Crashes on a bike are rarely serious and few involve the head— but, when they do, it's a sweaty situation. ☹ A helmet can help avoid a fracture or limit its seriousness, and even do the same for a brain injury. But it is only light protection... Watch out for the feeling of invulnerability* that protective equipment can give. The key thing is to ride without taking any risks.

I should really tattoo this sentence to my body, but I don't really like tattoos.

Must cover your entire forehead!

Hard shell which redistributes any impact and protects the life of the polystyrene.

Well-adjusted straps and retention system properly tightened!

Polystyrene absorbs even the slightest impact from any crash.

Most models come in several sizes.

Long hair? Don't put it up in a bun—it needs to go under the sides of the helmet. Some helmet retention systems are specifically designed to be able to put a ponytail through.

Plastic is fantastic! With time and exposure to sunlight, it loses its protective qualities and then—garbage can. See the manufacturers' recommendations on how long to use the helmet and don't go a maximum of one or two years beyond it.

A helmet's price has no impact on its reliability.

Take care—it's fragile!
As soon as a helmet receives any impact, it loses its protective qualities and must be replaced. So avoid placing it or attaching it anywhere where it might fall.

The lighter and airier a helmet is, the quicker you forget it once it's on your head. But the more stylish it is, the more you want to wear it, right?

*In newspeak, this is called "risk compensation."

BELL

(Legally required in some places)
Its little "ding ding" is so pleasant that few people actually react to it. Personally I prefer to warn of my passage with a cheerful exclamation of "Bike, bike!," which I accompany with a smile and a gesture of thanks.

A klaxon is funny if you're riding in a clown's outfit, but otherwise comes across as aggressive: honk hmmm...

MIRROR

Reassuring and practical! Handy for anyone, and essential for anyone who struggles to turn to look over their shoulder.
Models that are fixed to the end of a road handlebar are nice but difficult to keep in good condition.

BULL BAR

SAFETY WING REFLECTOR

To protect yourself from the annoyance of motorists who get too close.
Inconvenient when riding side by side with someone.

SMALL FLAG

Buy yourself one, or make your own using a metal pole and a couple of zip ties. Must be solid and well attached so as not to injure anyone!

BAGS, SADDLEBAGS,

OR HOW TO CARRY YOUR STUFF ON A DAILY BASIS

BACKPACK

Perfect for short trips

Everybody already owns one. Very practical once you're off the bike. It does make your back sweat a lot, and its weight is annoying if you opt for a sporty or racing riding position.
Same problem for the messenger bags used by certain bicycle couriers.

FANNY PACK   *"Hip bag"*

The best option if you want a small bag that stays on you. Worn on the hips—better than a purse, which is a hassle on a bike.

Available in volumes up to 5 liters and can also be used when traveling.

THE MOST IMPORTANT THING: THAT ANY BAG IS SAFELY SECURED AND KEPT CLOSED!!!

REAR PANNIERS

A cyclo-touring classic, also well suited for carrying around a load of stuff with you on a daily basis. Versions from German brands are great: durable, waterproof, simple, and practical attachment system.

Volume up to 2 x 25 liters

Riding with only one pannier, even if it's super-loaded, doesn't destabilize the bike once you're riding—other than slightly if you need to brake suddenly. But when traveling, be sure to balance weight left/right and front/rear.

The inside of a pannier can quickly become a bit shamboli. Using bags inside the bag can help you find stuff.

BASKET, CRATE, BOX

A metal basket is ideal, placed at the front or on the back. And a sturdy wooden crate or a plastic box can do the trick.

A regular plastic crate securely attached with zip ties, for example.

Steel wire basket attached to a luggage rack.

Exists as an all-in-one as well.

CLASSIC SADDLEBAG

A British specialty in waxed cotton, attractive, solid, waterproof, available in both large and small versions.

⚠️ Doesn't work for small frames—the rear wheel will touch the saddlebag.

Up to 25-liter capacity

Needs buckles at the back of the saddle or a specific attachment. Quick release supports and Carradice® SQR (Seatpost Quick Release) mean it can be adapted for urban usage, allowing it to be quickly removed or replaced. You can also strap it to the front, on the handlebars.

A PAIR OF LUGGAGE STRAPS

To fix anything to your luggage rack. Non-elastic straps with a buckle or a clip are much more secure than elastic straps or bungee cords.

Lightweight and don't take up too much space, so always handy to have with you.

LUGGAGE RACKS

FOR TRANSPORTING YOUR STUFF

REAR

THE CLASSIC

Easily forgotten about.
Models which allow you to hang panniers from them are a bit heavier but give a better (lower) center of gravity and reduce the instability that can be caused by bags that are overloaded.

Make sure to respect the maximum weight indicated for the rack.

SEATPOST LUGGAGE RACK

For bikes without eyelets from which a luggage rack can be attached. Limits the weight and type of panniers which can be used, plus ugly and a bit heavy… Those who have used bikepacking saddlebags report that they're a much better option.

FRONT

"PIZZA RACK"-STYLE FRONT RACK

With a good strap, it's perfect for attaching a basket, crate, or pretty much anything else (though you're limited in width if you have road handlebars).

FRONT LUGGAGE RACK

For carrying front panniers, which must be loaded with care (weight limited and balanced) so as not to make steering unsteady and demanding for the upper body. Carrying weight on the front of the bike puts more pressure on the shoulders and arms and creates more wind resistance. ☺

BIKEPACKING
FOR THE ADVENTURERS

Traveling light means you can ride harder routes and keep your bike running smoothly. There is a range of panniers that are a good match for this: easy to mount without a luggage rack, to carry travel equipment that is itself lightweight and compact. On the other hand, they aren't practical for carrying by hand nor easy to take on and off several times a day, and they can't carry very much. So a bit meh for grocery shopping and hanging out around town.

Saddlebag of 8- to 15-liter capacity, on top of which you can secure a raincoat or gilet

Frame-attached bag with around a 3-liter capacity, unsuitable for small frames because it'll prevent you from using your water bottle cages

Dry bag of around 5- to 10-liter capacity attached with a handlebar harness or with two straps

Two stem bags, each approximately 1-liter capacity

Top tube bag, around 1-liter capacity

Mini-pump and emergency inner tubes secured directly to the frame

Really convenient for keeping lots of useful things at hand: snacks, wallet, charger, repair kit, glasses case, pocketknife, sunscreen...

→ Certain frames can accommodate a third water bottle cage by having an extra one beneath the down tube—perfect for a tool-storage bottle.

→ On forks with threaded boltholes you can attach water bottle cages, or supports to carry panniers of around 3 or 4 liters in capacity.

Those who are handy with a sewing machine could make these bags at home, so long as the material used is thoroughly waterproof!

CHILDREN ON THE BIKE

BIKE SEATS FOR CHILDREN

Can be used from around nine months (or from as soon as the child can sit upright). Depending on the model they are either attached to the front of the bike (suitable for children up to 30 lbs) or the back (suitable for up to 50 lbs, so around four to five years of age). Seats attached to the seatpost are the most comfortable, because they pick up fewer of the vibrations from the road.

A sturdy kickstand is really handy!

Seats must be certified and come with a seat belt and foot rests.

Wearing a helmet is compulsory for children in many places, even if the child is just a passenger.

TRAILER

Suitable from around six months to up to about five years, and for one or two kiddos. Towing this sort of carriage requires gentle steering. Difficult to take on hilly or lively routes, or indeed on public transit, but can be left at school during the day.

CARGO AND LONG-TAIL

• Cargo bike: Suitable from babyhood when used with a car seat (or baby carrier), and for up to four little ones.
• Long-tail: No age limit and suitable for up to three children. Seriously cool, hardy, and very safe. Not easy to fit into your budget or your apartment.

THE KIDS HAVE GROWN UP SO QUICKLY! → p. 68 for a little introductory lesson

TAG ALONG

A half-bike attached behind the adult's machine: The child can pedal and get used to being on the road.

TOW BAR, FOLLOWME, AND TOW ROPES

The child can ride solo or be towed.

SKILLED AND ALERT ON THEIR OWN BIKE

Ready to ride under their own steam? They'll need to learn how to stay safe (pp. 76–81) and ideally have the responsible adult riding behind, talking to the child throughout so that they feel secure and accompanied.

BIKE BUS

For trips to school, under the same principles as a "walking bus." A nice scheme for a group of parents to set up, perhaps? And an excellent cycling school!

TANDEM

Great for cyclo-touring, particularly semi-recumbent versions.

MUDGUARDS

Invaluable for protecting yourself from spray on wet roads. The more they cover, the better.

They also protect the drivetrain a bit.

→ *increases its life*

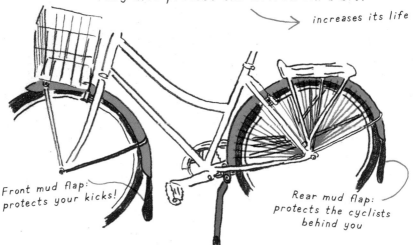

Front mud flap: protects your kicks!

Rear mud flap: protects the cyclists behind you

Mountain bike-specific mud guards offer less protection but avoid a buildup of mud that can jam the wheels.

At the front: to avoid having to eat too much mud

On a bike without eyelets or the necessary clearance* →*removable models*

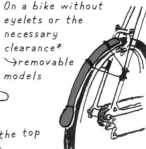

At the back: to spare the top of your buttocks

* The amount of space the tire has available to pass the chain stays, the seat stays, the brakes, and the fork

KICKSTAND

Really useful for impulsive stops, all while offering easy access to the bike, to panniers, to child seats... A center, two-leg kickstand is best.

SKIRT GUARD

A protective covering to avoid any risk of seeing your clothing (or a finger, or the ankle of a rear passenger) getting trapped in the spokes. #butchery

Most commonly seen on bikes in continental Europe as well as on bike-share bikes.

REPAIR KIT

"EVERYDAY" VERSION WHICH SHOULD
ALWAYS BE AT THE BOTTOM OF YOUR BAG

More complete, traveling version → p. 102

Good multi-tools with:
- Allen keys
- Flathead and Phillips screwdrivers
- Chain tool!

Mini-pump—
as mini as suits you

Reinflating wide tires with a mini-mini-mini pump is a real buzzkill!

Patching kit:
- 5–6 patches
- One tube of glue, in good condition
- Two plastic tire levers
- One small scraper

Tubeless kit:
- Puncture plugs
- Mini-file
- Installation tool

Emergency inner tube
Suited for your tire size!!!
(Both diameter and width)
A tube that's too narrow can still do the job

+ **Latex gloves**: Weigh nothing and useful to prevent your hands getting filthy while you are tinkering ✌

THINGS
—TO HAVE   AT HOME—

- Foot pump with pressure gauge
- Rags
- Degreaser
- Oil or wax chain lube

See p. 122 for the tools used by bike mechanics

AN OUTFIT THAT

HERE TOO, COMFORT SHOULD ALWAYS TAKE PRIORITY: GO FOR LIGHT, LOOSE, AND COMFORTABLE CLOTHES!

Jackets, gilets, zip-up sweats, and shirts are all great. You can completely unzip or unbutton them for full ventilation and to avoid feeling like you're in an oven.

Wool is best at dealing with sweat. A merino base layer will help regulate your body temperature, even when worn in summer. Unlike synthetic materials it doesn't transform sweat into an unpleasant smell, and it dries much quicker than cotton.

Choose a T-shirt that covers the top of your butt once you're leaning over on the bike, assuming you don't want to show off the color of your underwear or your plumber's crack.

GLOVES?

Cycling mitts protect your hands in the event of a fall—a likely outcome in mountain biking, rare in road cycling or bike commuting if you're riding with care. They also offer a small comfort boost.

CYCLING SHORTS?

(Shorts with padding, called chamois— pronounced "shammy")

Padded, designed for sport, and worn without underpants. Non-bib shorts are more practical, allowing for easier bathroom breaks and light shorts to be worn over them, for a more casual look and to have pockets. You can ride for hours or even days without needing to wear cycling shorts, so long as you have a comfortable position and saddle and a broken-in crotch. ☺

In these circumstances, the best option is merino boxers or trail running shorts.

SUITS (ME)

THE BASICS

Tight pants made from inflexible materials (skinny jeans, for instance) quickly wear out where they rub.

→ skirt guard p. 60

If wearing a long skirt, you can hold it shut with an elastic band or clip, or wear long and/or skintight shorts underneath.

ON YOUR PERIOD?

"When I'm on my period, I worry about discharge leaking from my panties. I use a moon cup, which I find practical when riding, and bring a long jumper or dark trousers with me." —Elisabetta, from Liège

For long journeys, period underwear is worth considering. Pads can cause rubbing and so irritation.

Bright colors are always a bright choice. Better than black at making you easily visible and allowing you to have a good day.

Open-toed sandals are OK, but no flip-flops, please!

Perhaps have an emergency rain jacket at the bottom of your pannier? It can also serve as a handy windbreaker if needed.

"CYCLING GEAR?"

You can be a cyclist without ever wearing cycling gear! It makes you look ridiculous, or pretentious, or unintentionally sexy (it depends), and all without making you go any faster. It's a uniform that's mainly useful for fitting in on Sunday morning rides among MAMILs (middle-aged men in Lycra).

OUTFITS FOR

IT'S RAINING!

• The "I'll wait until it passes" option: If it's a storm or it looks like it's just a shower, find yourself some shelter.

• The "To hell with it!" option: Take the plunge—"OK, let's go, it's not as if I'm made out of sugar"—and quickly dry yourself off when you get to your destination, having a change of clothes ready. OK for journeys that are neither too long nor too cold.

• The "GORE-TEX option": This means a "breathable" rain jacket, with ventilation holes under the arms. But this is no miraculous solution—if you're pushing hard on the pedals, you will steam up... Choose one that is large enough that it can be used in the winter, while wearing two layers underneath it, as well as in the summer. Cycling raincoats rarely have a hood—if you want one, you'll need to look at hiking jackets. Please try to find PFAS-free technical clothes.

• The "I'm cool under my poncho" option: Airy yet protective (even of the thighs), but greatly increases wind resistance and isn't very practical for steering. Can be stored under the saddle.

Waxed jackets and ones that are essentially plastic sheeting are no good. Condensation quickly builds within them, so as soon as you move you find yourself drenched from the inside...

Waterproof over-pants and over-shoes keep the bottom half of your outfit dry. Worth using if the forecast is very rainy.

+ a waterproof cap, a lifesaver for four eyes like me who haven't embraced contact lenses!

YOU'RE FREEZING YOUR BUTT OFF!

Even if it is absolutely freezing, you will warm up as soon as you get moving! You have to control your effort and use the right number of layers to avoid sweating too much (wet → cold → really, really not cool).

Staying warm when staying still ≠ staying warm when active! When cyclo-touring, you'll be good in temperatures as low as freezing with two or three layers—but always bring an extra one with you for when you take breaks!

You can set off a bit too bundled up, but be ready to stop and take off a layer once you've warmed up

A light cap or tube/neck scarf (Buff) underneath the helmet

Merino tube/ neck scarf (Buff)

Below freezing? Three-fingered "lobster" mittens, or ski gloves

Thick socks
Overshoes

EXAMPLES OF LAYERING COMBINATIONS

	59°F	46°F	32°F	23°F	5°F
Layer 1	Merino T-shirt, breathable top				
Layer 2	Woolen jumper, thick shirt, windbreaker, fleece	Down jacket, winter jacket, or very thick sweater	Woolen sweater, or fleece		
Layer 3			Down jacket, winter jacket		
Layer 4					Another jacket!?
Accessories	Middle-season gloves	Warm gloves, tube scarf, light hat	Extra-warm gloves, tube scarf, hat or balaclava, overshoes, heating pads…		

RIDING

Beginners won't remain that way for long! Once you get riding, you soon build up skill and a sense of security on the bike. You can always look at a cycling course or class to get off on the right foot, and take lessons to progress further.

No matter your level of experience there is always room to improve, and it's important not to become overly confident. Follow the example of the cat: always alert, controlled, and graceful.

Riding calmly is always the safest option and gives the best opportunity to appreciate what's around us.

It's also important to follow all rules of the road (except for rules that are actually unsafe for cyclists), for the benefit of everyone—we're riding on public roads and in shared spaces!

"You really have to keep in mind that people—pedestrians, drivers, whoever—don't see you, hardly see you, or only see you at the last minute. So don't hesitate to whistle, sound your bell, or look them in the eyes to make yourself visible."

—Marion, performance technician from Marseille

LEARN

IDEAL METHOD?
For getting started!

Not everyone has had the good fortune to have learned how to ride as a child, or to have cycled all their life... Confidence and dexterity on two wheels isn't innate!

① Learn how to __balance__ on two moving wheels with a balance bike, or strider — a bike with the pedals taken off. Leave the saddle low so that you can steady yourself with your feet.

② Familiarize yourself with __braking and cornering__. Increase distance and speed. Build up your confidence, with no pressure and no training wheels.

③ __Add pedals__ and see how they're used! Then, when you feel ready, sit in the saddle.

The size and weight of the bike, as well as its safety measures, count a lot for newbies!

Being held or pushed only gives the illusion of being able to balance— it's a skill better acquired solo. Encouraging words make a difference, but simply offering an attentive and reassuring presence is enough!

Get into the habit of wearing a helmet right from the very beginning (in many places they're compulsory for kids), but also gloves and knee pads if you're anxious.

HOP!

To get underway easily, choose an easy ("low") gear, especially if you're setting off on an uphill. The simplest way to move into an easier gear is to do so while pedaling and before stopping (→ see next page). Once stopped, you can move through two or three gears by lifting the back wheel off the ground and turning the pedals with your hand.

① While stopped: Get on the bike without getting into the saddle. Keep both feet on the ground and put both hands on the handlebars.

② Put the pedal you're going to push off with into the right position—about a quarter of the way down from the top.

③ Position your foot on the pedal, between the toe and the arch of your foot.

HOP!

CHECK!

HOP!

④ Go! Two birds with one stone—push down on the pedal to set off and to help you get up into the saddle.

Always look where you're going, while holding the handlebars neither too tightly nor too lightly and always being ready to brake.

<u>Pedaling</u> is simply pressing down on each pedal in turn. The best pedal stroke involves pushing down when a pedal is at the top until it reaches the bottom, while the non-pedaling leg does as little as possible.

CHANGE

HOW TO CHANGE YOUR PEDALING SPEED (CADENCE)

Three options for any given terrain:

① Use your legs to increase or decrease the speed at which you're pedaling.

②ₐ Change gear by shifting sprocket. The shifter lever on the right-hand side controls the rear derailleur.

③ₐ Change gear by shifting chainring. The left shifter controls the front derailleur. (In the UK, right and left shifters are opposite!)

<u>It's important to prepare to move into an easier gear</u> and not to find yourself grinding away at the bike like a fool at the point of shifting... Soft pedaling is less tiring, and the chain positions itself soooooo much better if you're gentle on the pedals at the point of changing gear.

What are these "gear" things? P. 11

Adjusting the derailleurs p. 118

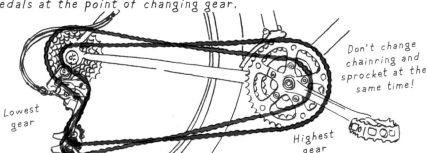

Don't change chainring and sprocket at the same time!

Lowest gear

Highest gear

②ᵦ Shift into an "easier" gear → move the chain up onto a larger sprocket, by increasing the tension on the rear derailleur cable.

③ᵦ Shift onto an "easier" chainring → move the chain down onto a smaller chainring by releasing the tension on the front derailleur cable.

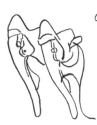

Gear shifters generally have two triggers: one that you push to stretch the derailleur up a notch, the other that you pull or push to slacken it a notch. On road and gravel bikes, these shifters are built into the brake levers.

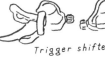

Trigger shifters

Grip shifters

GEAR

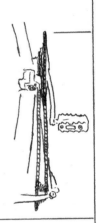

GOOD SPIN

To spare your beloved knees, and because
it doesn't make you go any faster, avoid
gear ratios that are too big. Grinding in a
big gear drains energy and risks cramps.
You need to find the cadence that suits
you and change gears so that you stay
at roughly that cadence, and can pedal
fluidly, throughout a ride.

SEEING WHICH GEAR YOU'RE IN

Some mountain bike gear shifters have marks on them
indicating the gears, but you can do without them
with a quick glance at the crankset and cassette.
Left-hand side, so biggest sprocket/small chainring,
is the easiest gear.
Right-hand side, so the reverse, is the biggest gear and
the most difficult—only to be used when descending.

CROSSING THE CHAIN IS BAD NEWS ☺

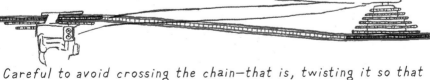

Careful to avoid crossing the chain—that is, twisting it so that
it's on an opposing chainring and sprocket (big chainring/big
sprocket or the reverse, small chainring/small sprocket). It puts
stress on the chain, damaging it, and can cause serious damage to
the derailleurs.

BRAKE

With mountain bike brake levers, you use one or two fingers to brake.

With modern road bike brake levers, you can still apply the brakes when on the tops (the higher part of the handlebar). But it's in the drops (the lower positions) that braking will be most effective and that you will have the best control.

REAR BRAKE OVER FRONT BRAKE, OR FRONT BRAKE OVER REAR?

☞ Use the two brakes in a simultaneous and gradual way. Perhaps go a little harder on the front brake than the rear…The front brake is the more powerful—only in corners and on slippery ground do you need to take care to use it gently. Have your weight on the saddle or toward the rear of the bike at the moment you brake.

On most bikes (though not in England and Italy), the front brake is linked to the left lever, the rear to the right lever.

EMERGENCY BRAKING

You need to practice this! The idea is to powerfully apply the brake to each wheel without locking them and while in a position that enables good control: leaning toward the back for stability and a low center of gravity. A skid is difficult to control—how difficult depends on your experience, speed, and the ground on which you're riding—and the loss of grip lengthens braking distance (eeekkk!). Changing direction too sharply can also destabilize the balance of the front wheel, and lead to a crash (ooffff…!).

Ineffective brakes? → p. 36

⚠️ Before braking to slow down, stop, or turn, check behind you to make sure there's no one coming up on you. If you're riding with several people, warn one another!

STOPPING

The best position once you've come to a stop: get out of the saddle and rest one or both feet flat on the ground.

If it's correctly adjusted, when in the saddle you won't be able to put anything other than the tip of one foot on the ground. This position isn't stable, nor comfortable, nor good for the crotch of your pants.

The acrobatic option: Stay perched in your saddle while leaning on an improvised crutch.

CORNERING

Anticipate the approaching bend and slow down before riding into it. If taking it at speed, stop pedaling and position the pedal that's on the inside of the bend so it's at the top.

Look where you are going, and not at your front wheel or anything else! You'll then naturally adopt the right steering to get you where you need to go.

Left hand bend: Don't cut the corner unless you can see all the way around it. Right hand bend: Go wide to carve a good, curving line. Once out of the bend and sure you're at enough of an upright angle that the pedal won't hit the ground, you can start pedaling again to optimize grip and benefit from the resulting momentum to keep your speed.

DESCENTS

Don't push it (or yourself). It takes time to gain confidence in going downhill, and that's OK.

The key thing is to stay in control of the bike (braking distances, lines, etc).

Anticipating when to brake and drawing good lines when taking corners helps.

A tire's grip is linked to the rubber it's made from, its width, its pressure, (p. 38) and its condition. Mountain bike-like treads on tires don't offer better grip when cornering on the road—the opposite, in fact.
Take extra care on roads that are soaking wet or in bad condition.

CLIMBING

Try to make yourself as light as a cat and to push down on the pedal as soon as the crank is pointing upward, without using too much force that you wear yourself out too quickly. The idea is to find a nice little rhythm of your own; one that is regular, suited to your capacity, lively enough to move you forward but while always keeping a little in reserve.

*Standing on the pedals allows you to get your momentum going again, to relax your body, or to get through a short, very steep section.
The heavier you are (accounting for the weight of the bike and your bags), the less you should do it so as to spare your knees.*

NEGOTIATING AN OBSTACLE

Butt out of the saddle, cranks parallel with the ground, body loose, and arms committed. When your front wheel hits the obstacle, shift your weight toward the back of the bike and then lift the wheel a little by pulling on the handlebars. Then shift your weight toward the front to lighten the back wheel, so easing its own passage over the obstacle.

1 or 2 inches is enough

"When there are cobblestones or the road is uneven, I lift myself out of the saddle, like a steadicam: Around me things move and shake, but me not so much."—Betta, from Liège

ON THE TRAILS!

Requires skill, good physical condition, and great care:

→ Always seek out the best lines by inspecting the obstacles ahead, all the while checking where your wheels are positioned so as to smoothly avoid current obstacles. The aim is to not take any unnecessary risks for yourself or your bike, nor to lose too much speed.

→ Get your butt out of the saddle frequently, to rest both it and your wheels, tires, and back.

→ Cushion the vibrations with your entire body and most notably with your arms and back, which should neither be too tense nor too relaxed.

→ It's exhausting. And when it gets scary, sing—it helps you relax!

Learning to ride hands-free is great for the confidence! It also helps you realize just how much the buttocks and the pelvis are involved in steering.

A FOCUSED YET COOL ATTITUDE

Everyone has to find a balance between relaxation and concentration when riding a bike, particularly if mixing with the traffic of a town. Your riding has to be alert and calm at the same time, with arms (for braking and steering) and legs (for acceleration) remaining ready to respond to surprises. *NB: Crashes in towns are relatively rare (though there's still a lot of work to be done to improve infrastructure), but you'll be much more likely to avoid serious injury if you ride at a gentle speed and with great care. Other vehicles' reduced speed in built-up areas also helps a lot. The conflation of motorcycle accidents with bicycle accidents is unhelpful and misleading.*

ACCOMPANIED AT FIRST

To get off to a good start and to gain confidence, you can ask an experienced cycling friend to accompany you on a daily journey. It's a chance for you to figure out the best route together, and to observe your friend's habits and ask lots of questions...

Many cycling associations offer lessons for beginners of any age. A good tip for maintaining the concentration, clarity (and enjoyment) that can be eroded during a routine journey.

IMPORTANT PRECAUTIONS

Pay attention to blind spots!

They can be a cause of fatal accidents for cyclists in towns, hence the importance of stopping *IN FRONT* of vehicles at red lights and stop signs.

Catch the eyes of drivers when you're

negotiating crossroads or roundabouts, to ensure that they have indeed seen you!
Even if you have priority, remain vigilant when cutting across the path of a vehicle, which can lead to serious accidents.

Don't press too close to a parked car, but—assuming there is

no danger—do move well to the right when being overtaken by a moving one. It's intimidating to be overtaken by, or even brushed by, a vehicle that's much faster and significantly heavier than you, but very few crashes are linked to being overtaken.

Rule of the road: When overtaking a cyclist, the gap between them and your vehicle should be at least 3 ft when in built-up areas and at least 5 ft in non-built-up areas. Like fierce dogs, us cyclists bite otherwise!

To protect against collisions from poorly timed door openings, try to look out for drivers in parked or idling vehicles.

Listening to music through earbuds or on headphones dramatically reduces the ability to pay attention and our perception of dangers.

Doing so is often banned for drivers.

RULES OF THE ROAD

Even though rules of the road were invented to prevent drivers from killing people, they also apply to cyclists and help protect them.

Compulsory: Varies by location, but often a bell, front and rear light, reflectors (including on the wheels), helmets for children.

Highly recommended: At night in built-up areas, reflective vest and headlamp.

Bike lanes:

There are designated bike-only lanes BIKE LANE and scenic or BIKE ROUTE low-traffic routes recommended for cyclists. Bikes are vehicles like any others, and so allowed on all roads unless there is this.

Always overtake on the left

Drivers hardly ever look in their right-side mirrors, and blind spots are dangerous.

Clearly indicate when changing direction

(especially when turning left!), and possibly when you're stopping too. These should be the only times you allow yourself to have just one hand on the handlebar.

How much stopping distance you need to leave to allow

for an emergency stop varies, depending on the quality of your brakes, tires, reflexes, the condition of the road...

Drinking and riding: Same limit as for others controlling vehicles, .08%. Drunkenness slows your reflexes, and its euphoric effect leads to taking stupid and dangerous risks.

In the event of an infraction (running a red, being on the phone while riding, riding on the sidewalk) there is the risk of a fine, but not points.

Insurance is not required on e-bikes that are limited to a speed of 28 mph.

Personal liability coverage on your homeowners or renters insurance may cover you if you find yourself responsible for a crash or if your bike is pilfered. → p. 87 for what to do in the event of an accident

DEDICATED BIKE LANES

Dedicated bike lanes separated from traffic are the surest way of avoiding several crash risks. Bike lanes on roads are good too.

That said, they are far from all being well conceived. Some are too narrow, forcing you to mount curbs, or have random interruptions. A bike lane like this can be great for cycling with children but a nuisance for trying to get somewhere at a steady pace. Depending on your confidence and speed, and despite notable risks (especially at night and in non-built-up areas), riding among the rest of the traffic can sometimes seem preferable and—aside from certain exceptions*—is allowed.

— * In the absence of dedicated bike lanes, choose the route that has the least traffic possible—even if it means making little detours along the way. → p82

Increasing the number of dedicated bike lanes remains crucial to helping as many people as possible feel safe using their bikes.

Plus having more places to park bikes securely!

Cycling associations are very active in these public interest campaigns.

Support them!

Roads that are one-way only for motor vehicles but on which cyclists can travel in both directions may seem dangerous, but it actually makes motorists travel more slowly on these streets. Crashes are no more common on these routes than on others.

COURTEOUS RELATIONS

• The slower and more fragile we are, the more priority we have.
It's cool to be understanding of, and well intentioned to, pedestrians,
Rollerbladers, those on scooters, and to slower cyclists!

• Stopping to let pedestrians cross a road disrupts your
momentum. In many cases, you can just slow down and negotiate
around them while giving plenty of space.
According to the rules of the road, though, you are generally obliged to stop.

• Sounding your bell or offering a friendly little exclamation ("Watch
your back; coming through!" or "Hi!") is a tactful way of making
sure you're noticed. Avoid using a klaxon or an aggressive tone.

• A powerful headlamp can give a feeling of security but
doesn't offer the best visibility in a well-lit, built-up area.
The reverse, in fact—it can dazzle and break the concentration
of any driver approaching you head on. In some places,
blinking headlights are banned.

> AS A GENERAL RULE, SET ASIDE ANY INCLINATION
> YOU MAY HAVE TO BE IN-YOUR-FACE. ♡

DON'T BE WORRIED ABOUT BEING A BOTHER!

Roads are public, and are for cyclists as much as they are for cars, buses, taxis, motorcycles... If a vehicle puts you under pressure, remain confident and sure of yourself. You don't have to ride in the gutter or mount the sidewalk, and you're not responsible for the anger or stress of certain drivers.

These instances of aggression can happen more or less anytime, but I put them into perspective by reminding myself that only a very small percentage of road users behave in a dangerous and irresponsible manner.

ASSERTING YOURSELF WITH DANGEROUS VEHICLES

• Don't hug the right-hand side of the road.

• Ride in the middle of the road, lifting your left arm to announce that you are going to turn in that direction.

• Stop in front of motor vehicles at traffic lights.

• When a vehicle is getting too close to your tail, adopt slightly odd steering, zigzagging slightly in the middle of the vehicle's path... Then go back into "normal" mode and ride toward the right as soon as it starts to overtake. A mirror really helps with this technique.

• If you're really worried about aggressive vehicles, use a safety flag on your bike to help keep them at a distance.

All these behaviors make us more visible and force drivers to take more care by increasing their distance and taking their foot off the gas.

RIDING OUTSIDE

Taking the time to plot good routes is fundamental to having a good time once in the saddle. We're looking for back streets and perhaps even for some trails or detours to uncover. Whatever makes the journey most exciting, pleasant, and safest!

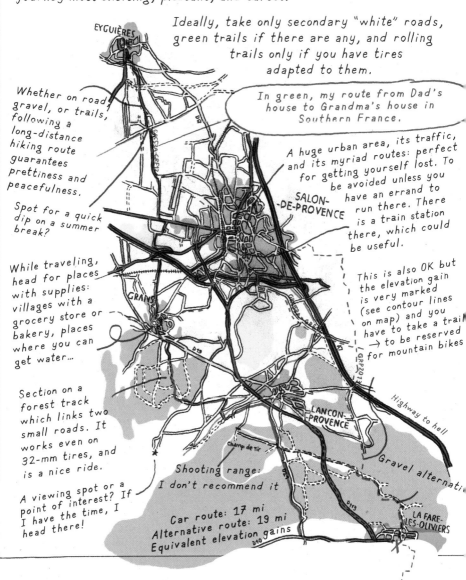

Ideally, take only secondary "white" roads, green trails if there are any, and rolling trails only if you have tires adapted to them.

In green, my route from Dad's house to Grandma's house in Southern France.

Whether on road, gravel, or trails, following a long-distance hiking route guarantees prettiness and peacefulness.

Spot for a quick dip on a summer break?

While traveling, head for places with supplies: villages with a grocery store or bakery, places where you can get water...

Section on a forest track which links two small roads. It works even on 32-mm tires, and is a nice ride.

A viewing spot or a point of interest? If I have the time, I head there!

A huge urban area, its traffic, and its myriad routes: perfect for getting yourself lost. To be avoided unless you have an errand to run there. There is a train station there, which could be useful.

This is also OK but the elevation gain is very marked (see contour lines on map) and you have to take a trail → to be reserved for mountain bikes

Highway to hell

Gravel alternati

Shooting range: I don't recommend it

Car route: 17 mi
Alternative route: 19 mi
Equivalent elevation gains

EYGUIÈRES

SALON-DE-PROVENCE

GRANS

LANCON-PROVENCE

Champ de tir

LA FARE-LES-OLIVIERS

URBAN AREAS

PRINTED MAP

The nicest way to prepare and visualize a route, but not very practical once on the road. Even with a map holder on the handlebars, it's not easy to read a map while riding and you have to stop regularly to unfold and refold it.

HOMEMADE ROAD BOOK

A list of roads, towns, and villages you'll join up along the way, intersections you mustn't miss... To be laminated with Scotch tape and wrapped around the handlebars. Cheap and practical.

GPS PHONE APP

To plot bike-friendly routes. Take care—they're just algorithms!
→ Strava, Komoot, RideWithGPS, Trailforks...
→ Many apps allow for turn-by-turn audio cues.
→ The bike routes suggested by Google Maps are dangerous and often crappy and illogical.
→ Maps.me is good for viewing maps offline.

A backup battery or charger may be necessary for self-sufficiency, even when riding with your phone in airplane + battery-saving mode + with the screen on the minimum brightness setting.

GPS BIKE COMPUTER

Handy devices for long journeys and for traveling. Waterproof and solid, good battery life, perfect at locating where you are, but one more high-tech and non-recyclable gadget.
GPS devices for hikers can also do the job.

CAARREEFUL!

Risks seem less omnipresent outside built-up areas, but crashes here are a bit more dangerous than those in towns. **Remain focused and calm!**

RIDING TWO ABREAST

Riding two abreast is often legal if you're not impeding traffic. When passing a vehicle from behind on narrow roads or at night, single file is recommended. To make overtaking easier, riding in single file is recommended on narrow roads, when a vehicle is approaching from behind, and at night.

IN ONE LARGE GROUP

Really not recommended = groups of more than 10 cyclists—on narrow roads, they can be very difficult to overtake and push certain drivers to make decisions that are a danger to everyone.

When there are lots of you, it's better to split into several small groups.

DOGS!

Some don't like intruders and like those on weird steeds even less.

Don't add to their dislike by staring them in the eyes. The small number of options if you are attacked:

☞ Fleeing option: Outrun the animal if it seems to have the weaker legs out of the two of you, and if the road lends itself to it (descent, tailwind). Many dogs only bark and defend when in front of their property, and don't run far or for long.

☞ Lay down the law option: Stop, address the animal sharply and calmly (no big movements)—"Get back!" "Go home"... Then, without panicking, set off again.

☞ Self-defense option: Get off your bike and use it as a barrier, or grab a long stick, to keep the animal at a distance.

☞ Primate option: Climb a tree (or on top of a car) and shout until someone comes to your aid.

TRRRUUUCCCKKK!

Be wary of the blast of air created when a large vehicle passes—it can be surprising, and even destabilizing. The same is true of certain gusts of wind. Plus they mess up your hair. ☺

RIDING ALL YEAR ROUND

IT'S USUALLY FINE!

Exposure to the elements is part of the pleasure of cycling, but also leads to reluctance about getting down to it. Luckily, you'd be surprised how long the good-cycling-weather seasons actually last—even in notoriously foul-weather places like Buffalo!

WIND

The worst, without doubt. What better than a gale or cold northerly wind in your face to make you hate cycling? It requires a good dose of sacrifice and zen. If possible: Ride with others in single file, find a "sheltered" route (trees, buildings), adopt a crouched position on the bike (aero bars are good for this), or treat yourself to a train or bus ticket.

This is the ONE situation in which I allow myself to wear headphones or earbuds. The noise of the wind is mind-numbing and stops me from hearing anything anyway.

RAIN

With a plan and a suitable outfit (p. 64), and ideally mudguards as well, it's fine. Be careful of the reduced grip on saturated roads, and heightened danger on manhole covers, pedestrian crossings, cobblestones, dead leaves... Worn tires don't help. ☺

COLD

Nothing that's insurmountable with the right outfit (p. 65). The first five minutes—the time it takes you to warm up—require a bit of motivation.

Watch out for black ice! Especially if you come across a sign that says "WATCH FOR ICY ROADS," or damp corners that aren't exposed to sunlight.

And what about snow? It requires maximum care and tires that are slightly underinflated and studded. Depending on the type of snow (soft, melting, icy) and the quantity, it might be best left to mountain bikers.

Even with the greatest care, and all possible experience and expertise, _it can happen._

Rather than trying to prevent a fall at all costs when you feel it coming, instead aim for a smooth roll, protecting your head and pushing your bike away from you.

You can be knocked out and lack clear thinking in the moment after a crash, so it's good to "prepare" for it...

No matter the type of crash, __take a moment to gather yourself and evaluate your injuries.__ Depending on how serious they are, call for help and/or take yourself to the nearest pharmacy or house

Ready to set off again? Check your bike before remounting. A wheel might have become bent, the seatpost off-kilter, the frame broken... Perhaps it would be more prudent to set back off on foot?

Did the crash involve another person and has it caused any damage? If the other vehicle involved is motorized, __make a report*__ or exchange contact details to progress an insurance claim.** Handling the matter informally between the two of you is likely to be disadvantageous.

*No matter who is at fault, in a crash with a motorized vehicle it is their insurance policy on which the claim is made. Helmet or not, e-bike (speed restricted) or not, our rights are the same.

**Cyclists might be covered by homeowners or renters insurance.

If the other party flees the scene or if you're the only one hurt, compensation may be available—but it'll be more complicated, including filing a police report, and then pursuing legal action or filing a claim.

__Coming to terms with any trauma:__ It can be difficult to return to the bike following a fall. The time it takes to regain confidence varies. For some, confidence comes from getting back in the saddle as quickly as possible. Others get there very gradually—maybe first being accompanied by friends, to turn this resumption into a celebration! Giving your bike a thorough service, and possibly changing certain pieces of equipment, can bolster its reliability and the confidence you have in it.

MOBILITY, HEALTH, SAVINGS, JOY, TRAVEL

☞ Using a mode of transport that benefits your physical and mental health and doesn't harm the world around us—in fact, does quite the opposite!

☞ Saving time and money
Including, for example, the time and money necessary to own and use a car and deal with everything that goes with it

☞ Riding with other cyclists for fun, whatever level they're at, and leaving the patriarchy in the gutter

☞ Learning how to make (mixed-mode transport) cocktails

☞ And why not grab your bike to go to a meeting 25 miles away, to visit with an aunt who lives one day of trekking away, or to reunite with a crush who lives at the other end of the country?

"Sometimes bad weather, tiredness, or a big climb along the way mean I can't be bothered to take my bike to get to my destination... In the end, I'm often too up against the clock to go on foot and, once on the bike, it's magical! The effort is nice, you get some air, and you feel in harmony with your bike and the town."

—Marion, sometimes depressed, sometimes badass, always busy

EXERCISE AND

PHYSICAL ACTIVITY IS NOT TO BE EQUATED WITH PERFORMANCE, SUFFERING, OR THE QUEST FOR A SUMMER BODY!

Nor with skintight getups made from petroleum-sourced fabrics

Cycling is indeed exercise, even when riding at a gentle pace, and only occasionally, and on a comfortable bike, even an electric one. It doesn't really make you lose weight, but:

- It helps reduce levels of body fat.

- It increases flexibility, joint mobility, bone health, posture, coordination, improves breathing, and bolsters the immune system.

- It releases serotonin, dopamine, and oxytocin, the hormones of well-being and happiness, woot woot!

"Move, move, move!," healthcare professionals urge: long live walking and cycling. These modes of "active travel" decrease the risks associated with sedentary lifestyles, which are a highway to cardiovascular disease, obesity, diabetes, high blood pressure, and cancer.

Even in town, where exposure to pollution is more marked during physical effort, the health equation remains abundantly positive!

It is a health equation that only changes in older age. Sight and balance problems make cycling dangerous, even if tricycles and balance bikes for adults do exist and are good tools for remaining mobile.

The bike is an opportunity to introduce physical activity to your day-to-day life and to your leisure time.

Doesn't that make more sense than taking a motorized vehicle to play sports in electricity-intensive buildings or in natural spaces that could do without a mass of visitors?

"I understood that I didn't need to be a great athlete to be able to use the bike as my travel method in town, even if, at first, Marseille scared me with its hills. The feeling of freedom that the bike gives me is much more intense than the one I feel in a car."

—Nathalie, osteopath and yoga teacher

The word "sport" originated in England in the 19th century and comes from the Old French word "desport," a synonym for "fun."

even if that isn't the subject of this book ☺

The bike can offer an exhilarating sporting experience. In developing physical endurance, the body releases endorphins—excellent for mental and emotional well-being, stress reduction, and for concentration.

During certain intense efforts, the body of a cyclist can even generate a lovely cocktail of endorphins and endocannabinoids! #runnershigh #longlivehomemadehighs

FOR THE PUBLIC GOOD

The bike isn't just a blast for the individual.
Its qualities benefit better living as a society!

Evaluation of the space needed for different modes of transport. See "The arrogance of space" by Mikael Colville-Andersen.

It is silent and takes up very little public space, whether in circulation or parked and stationary. It can very easily live alongside pedestrians, with little risk.

It contributes to a reduced demand for energy.

Its use is nonpolluting, which benefits all living beings.

The bike is admittedly limited in its ability to transport large loads (assuming you don't have a cart) and for daily journeys of more than about 15 miles, but in most cases it's a vehicle suited, perhaps even ideally, to built-up areas. Making it your primary mode of transport leads to shopping at small stores and markets and counters urban sprawl.

And while costing you much less than owning your own car (meaning you can treat your buddies to a round more often), the bike also saves money for society.

• Health and social security savings: in preventing a whole heap of illnesses (cardiovascular...) and in benefiting emotional well-being.
• Infrastructure savings: in its light demands on roads, parking spots, and security arrangements—which cyclists and pedestrians also help finance.

And what do you know? If you feel better in body and mind, and if you buy drinks for your buddies, life is beautiful!

Yes, when you push down a little on the pedals—no matter your level of fitness and body type—you are going to sweat.
But, perhaps it's time to come to terms with perspiration and with the body's whiffs!

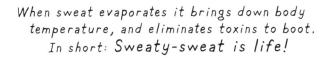

When sweat evaporates it brings down body temperature, and eliminates toxins to boot. In short: Sweaty-sweat is life!

Even so, we need to take care not to be too antisocial and not to give fuel to the anti-cycling fire... "It's too difficult!" "It's not appropriate for getting to work!" "You really have to be an athlete..." yada yada yada.

Depending on your metabolism and on the arrival of heatwaves, sweat can start dripping from you—even when you're not overdoing it—and become an annoyance. There's no miraculous solution. It would equally be annoyance on public transit, in a car without AC, or even on foot.

You can carry a toiletry bag with you (washcloth, soap, small towel) and a clean T-shirt, the ideal being to have access to a shower when you arrive.

Deodorant hack: Moisten your armpits with a little bit of coconut oil (it prevents irritation) and then talc them with regular baking soda: an antibacterial, it absorbs odors effectively.

If you are certain you're going to sweat, a merino top is more comfortable than a cotton one.

Antiperspirant hacks: Set off early so you don't have to hurry, and avoid non-breathable duds or those that are too heavy for the weather. Leaving the day before, in your birthday suit and without a backpack, is ideal! Not going too fast also means you prolong cycling's main benefit: putting you into a good mood.

RIDING

WITH CYCLING BUDDIES

What a delight to share treks, cyclo-touring trips, or even just short rides with friends. Camaraderie and passion for cycling are often reinforced coming out of such a trip, assuming of course you're not throwing yourself into a challenge that's too hardcore. When preparing a trek, the most experienced can take care of planning the route—while considering everyone's individual concerns and abilities.

If in doubt, keep it simple.

WITH YOUNG CHILDREN

Kids love spending time outside with their cherished adults as their pilots or as their guides!

There is no weather forecast that can put them off, nor much else, and their words of encouragement are as amusing as they are galvanizing!

WITH PEOPLE WITH DISABILITIES

There are adapted bikes that offer the opportunity to get active in the fresh air! They are available from specialist organizations. Why not get started with:

• A classic tandem? To ride with someone who has sight problems or who can't steer.

• A semi-recumbent tandem? These have a seat at the front from which you can have a great time without needing to steer, and can choose whether or not to pedal—potentially with hand pedals rather than ones pushed with the feet.

TOGETHER

WITH NEW CYCLISTS, or with someone who is getting back on the bike following a crash:

Show care and attention! Be encouraging without exaggerating, appreciate the progress they have made rather than focusing on the things they can't do, ride in a laid-back way and without showing off, pay attention to the needs and the difficulties of the other person. We are all different when learning to ride a bike, and it's harder for some than it is for others... But, ultimately, everyone can have a great time!

WITH A ROMANTIC PARTNER ♥

Going cyclo-touring with a partner isn't necessarily easy and can increase tensions equally effectively as it can affection. It depends on the arrangements made at the start of the trip and the care you take to talk and listen to one another.

WITH "RACERS"

The most stimulating option if you want to progress or if you're on a mission to better yourself. But you have to know how to listen to your body, to not place the bar too high, and to regularly repeat the same mantra to yourself: _fun and safety first!_ Along the way you'll learn techniques to communicate about hazards while riding quickly in a single file pack.

WITH ANIMALS

A basket is perfect for carrying around a small animal, or a trailer for a big doggy. Unless your dog wants to take the lead and pull you along? → Canine mountain biker!

— # TRANSPORTATION

The main advantage of the car is undoubtedly its ability to cover a whole range of needs without having to worry about organizing anything.
If you want to do without it, you have to learn to concoct your own "cocktails"...
There are plenty of recipes with the bike as an ingredient!

JUST THE BIKE

First, it must be said that the best bicycle cocktail might be a "straight shot"! Roll up to your destination, no transfers necessary. Finally, the US is making headway to make this choice possible, from protected bike lanes and urban trails to regional greenway networks. Travel by bike is getting easier and more convenient, yet there's much more work to be done to make it the safest, most practical option for most people, from "road diets"—reconfiguring lanes for motor vehicles into lanes for bicycles—to pedestrian plazas, neighborhood greenways, bike-share and car-share programs, single-lane roundabouts (which, studies show, slow traffic down, reduce travel time and pollution, and dramatically reduce the injury-causing crashes common at intersections), and mixed-use development that shrinks the city and brings businesses back within biking distance after decades of soul-sucking sprawl.

BIKE + TRAIN

In Europe, passenger rail is a key form of transport, well connected and covering most areas. In the US, the car craze had the effect of dismantling what was once a good passenger rail system, which is just now starting to regrow and reconnect. Amtrak is the main passenger rail company in the US, with only a few minor private or public systems. Some Amtrak trains allow bikes to go on board, in designated storage spaces. Other trains might have rules that vary by route, day, or time. Sometimes a bike might need to be boxed (a pain) while other times the bike can just roll on board (a joy). And speaking of trains, Rails to Trails Conservancy (or, shall we hope, Rails with Trails) dreams of a country-wide bike system. Support their efforts if you can!

COCKTAILS

BIKE + BUS

A recipe with an uncertain outcome… Depending on your destination, you may find not trains but city or coach buses. To store a bike in the luggage hold of a coach bus, there has to be space and goodwill from the operating company (some have it) and the driver (some don't). And some city buses have bike racks on their front bumpers—helpful if you're able to ride some but not all of your trip, or if you live far from the nearest bus stop.

Depending on your preferred cocktail recipe, buying a folding bike may be a good idea.

BIKE + CAR

• **The between-friends recipe**: If you don't have access to your own car, you could keep a <u>bike rack</u> at home and occasionally piggyback a trip in a friend's car when they're on their way to somewhere—even when the trunk is full!

• *The never-the-same-twice recipe*: <u>Hitchhiking!</u> As most cars only travel with one or two people in them, folding down the back seat to welcome a human and their bike is doable! It's also the ultimate way to get back to civilization in the event of a technical failure in the middle of nowhere.

The safest tactic: Place yourself at the edge of a built-up area, thumb in the air and with an unforced smile, in front of a space in which a car would be OK to park. Don't make a sign saying which direction you're looking to go in… Wait until a person stops to exchange a couple of words and ask where they're headed. If you have any sense that something is off, you can say: "Ah, damn, that's not where I'm going." Bad experiences with hitchhiking are rare, but even so…

BIKE + BOAT

Yes! And usually free! Great for island-hopping vacations.

BIKE + AIRPLANE

Oh, what a shame—I've not got much space to talk abo
It's doable—you have to package up your bike with m
you want it to arrive in a rideable state. There i
option to pack it only lightly thinking the bagga
might take more care as a result. First off, you

EXPANDING THE TRAVELS

Travels by bike can be seen as an obvious extension of riding for practicality's sake—a shift away from cycling as a leisure activity and toward a more meaningful experience and, of course, an adventure in and of itself.

Whether you're a daily cyclist, cycle only occasionally, are a sporting cyclist, or just in good condition and motivated, with a suitable bike and a bit of organization there are no limits.

"In traveling by bike, whether during my vacations or just in my daily life, I've developed a strong sense of mobility. Traveling everywhere by bike, no matter the season and carrying everything I need with me, gives me a new perspective on our relationship with the energy that fuels our transport, our homes, our infrastructures. Being a cyclist transforms my relationship with travel and enables me to remove the superfluous from my life."
—Alizée Depin, artist, editorial designer, and mountain enthusiast

POSSIBILITIES: BY BIKE

The limits aren't imposed by mileage, or elevation gains, or hours in the saddle, even if these are the numbers that lead to trepidation when starting a trip and satisfaction at the end of it. They're also not a matter of physical condition. In taking our time and listening to our bodies, we can all surprise ourselves by pedaling for a long time and a long way. There is no point in hurting yourself and seeking to compare your performance to top-level athletes'.

Rather, the limits are mental ones—you need desire, humility, and boldness. That's why, were I to offer just one piece of advice: Never forget to ride for pleasure, to live in the moment, and savor the beautiful countryside and the people and nature you encounter along the way.

This surpassing of limits increases your self-confidence, which mixes with a taste for freedom that establishes itself as soon as you set foot outside your door, a well-being that you gain with activity and fresh air, and a peaceful relationship with the seasons and the land. With every mile, the surprise of "being there" is renewed.

THE "MINI-ADVENTURE" PLAN

There is no minimum time or distance for a trip by bike—it's the spirit in which the journey is undertaken which is most important. You throw yourself into adventure as soon as you spend one night away from home.

"Just one night?" It's the perfect way to play hooky for a day but also good for testing out your cycle-camping gear and getting to know your buddies in trekking mode, before you dream up and prepare longer trips together.

Trying a ride of between 30 to 60 miles in one or two sections allows you to get familiar with your bike when loaded with gear—and so notably heavier, which especially makes itself felt when climbing. Pay extra attention to riding a comfortable rhythm, staying hydrated, and taking frequent breaks.
This test run also allows you to gain confidence in your gear and to tell yourself that perhaps you don't need all that many things to enjoy days in the outdoors—bivouac and spend a nice night in the wilderness.

Some Yanks call this plan the "S240"—sub-24-hour overnight

THE "TRAVELING LIGHT" PLAN

Carrying bivouac gear, all-climate clothes, a few provisions, and a book—the idea of "autonomy" on a trip is joyful.
But if you don't want to ride a heavy bike, aren't a fan of camping (particularly solo) or don't have equipment at hand, want to get a feel for bike travels before investing more money, or just like being pampered on your arrival, you can also stay in <u>a home or hotel overnight.</u>

By planning stops at the homes of friends and family, at those of Warmshowers hosts (warmshowers.org) or in small hotels, you can set off without the tent/sleeping bag/air mattress/ pot-stove pack, without large supplies of food or water, and you can easily wash your duds. You will sleep well, following a hot shower and a friendly meal.

You can also set off with bikepacking bags (→ p.57) and a <u>limited, light, and compact collection</u> of essentials:

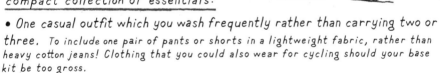

• *One casual outfit which you wash frequently rather than carrying two or three.* *To include one pair of pants or shorts in a lightweight fabric, rather than heavy cotton jeans! Clothing that you could also wear for cycling should your base kit be too gross.*

• *In the summer and between seasons: Three layers for the upper body is enough, with the combination depending on conditions (→ p. 65). Example: one light sweater + one compact down jacket + 1 rain jacket.*

• *One sleeping bag liner—much more compact than a sleeping bag itself and, by protecting your hosts' linens, allows you to be a considerate guest.*

Two more tips for luck:
→ I don't bring books or magazines with me... I read whatever I find on the premises!
→ I send myself parcels to be picked up along the way, either to friends' homes or using general delivery. The pleasure of traveling light is worth the cost of posting an outfit for a party or something I need for work.

THE REPAIR KIT

A whole heap of technical glitches and booboos can be sorted out along the way, but you need the stuff to patch things up!

This list supplements the everyday kit (p. 61) with its *mini-pump* and reliable *multi-tools* equipped with a chain tool.

Complete puncture kit:

• 2 or 3 new emergency inner tubes
• Three plastic tire levers (sometimes you break one)
• 10 to 15 patches in a range of sizes
• Two tubes of tire patch glue, in good condition
• Two scrapers (often sandpaper)
• Four to five pieces of old tire or tire repair patches

For tubeless punctures:

• Cleaning and plug insertion tools + about 10 plugs + spare valve and valve cores + a quality valve core removal tool + Presta valve adapter for air compressor

To fix other hassles:

• 6 pairs of chain links and quick link
• Spoke key (found on certain multi-tools)
• Small bottle of oil or of wax chain lube
• Small cutting pliers and pocketknife
• Brake pads, spare brake, and gear cables
• A roll of duct tape + needle and strong thread for repairs

First aid kit:

disinfectant, gauze dressings and/or wound-healing gel with compression and regular bandage, chamois cream, wintergreen essential oil (good for massaging muscles and joints), pain reliever, tick-removal tweezers, antiseptic wipes, and medical tape

+ 1 lucky charm

GOOD ADVICE FROM FRIENDS

"→ No need for a state-of-the-art bike to set off on a road trip. It's mainly a case of finding a rhythm and pacing your efforts.
→ Don't forget about regular breaks and never ride in a hurry.
→ Don't ignore the heat and try riding at night—it's awesome!
→ Wrap your things in plastic bags—they're perfect for keeping things dry.
→ Cycling sunglasses are incredible! Goodbye dust, midges, headaches...
→ Putting some herbs in your water bottle stops you tasting the plastic.
→ When you're getting started, 30 miles with 2,000 feet of elevation gain is enough."

—Caroline Decque, professional forager and adventurer

"If you know a woman who wants to take to the road alone on her bike, or on foot, or on horseback—be kind. Don't make her carry your worries, because you risk taking the wind from the sails of a beautiful desire for solo escape with the cop-out that 'you're never safe from a bad encounter.' Encourage her! Advise her to find safe spots for sleeping outside. Give her a good light so she can ride safely at night. A down jacket, gloves, or even an emergency survival blanket."
—Marion Mériguet,
"Lay down your gun,"
veloculte.com

"If I go out alone on my bike, I wouldn't know how to repair it or check it... I'd like to be sure that it's working well and that it's not dangerous."
—Aimée, a spirited Quebecois, now settled in Marseille for a decade

MAINTENANCE & SMALL REPAIRS

The peace of mind of being prepared for a whole range of situations that could show up along the way accompanies the sense of freedom on a bike. One such uncool situation: something breaking among your gear. Usually, these problems can be resolved with a spirit of resourcefulness and two or three easy-to-carry tools (p. 102). That said, being able to repair a puncture and maintain your brakes is non-optional. ☺

The mechanics of bikes can seem like an unscalable mountain to newbies, but relax—to get started, you don't need a desire to know everything there is to know. The best way of learning is often by tinkering alongside someone who knows what they're doing. Is there perhaps a cooperative shop in your area that is friendly and guards against mansplaining? Or a keen individual who is in a position to be able to teach you everything you'd like to know? Video tutorials are also helpful.

In any case, these next few pages—or those within more comprehensive mechanical manuals—are useful for an initial overview of technical stuff, or for refreshing your memory.

CHAIN CARE

To work effectively and to not wear out prematurely—taking with it the cassette and chainring(s)—this drivetrain centerpiece must remain clean, lubricated, and in good condition.

This is a maintenance job that needs doing more often than a complete bike clean. Generally when the chain needs lubrication, it will make itself heard!

CLEANING/DEGREASING

• If using oil lubricant: a bike-specific degreasing product, or kerosene/paraffin.
• If using wax lubricant, hot water and dish soap is sufficient.

When the chain doesn't leave any (black) dirt on your fingers, that's when it's clean.

While you're at it, use a small flathead screwdriver to remove the grime and dirt that collects on the rear derailleur pulleys.

Just a little drop of oil or wax is enough, and only on the inside of the chain.

Check wear and tear on the chain and change it as needed. → p. 116

LUBRICATION

Once the chain is completely dry, apply <u>chain oil</u> while moving through all the links by turning the pedals by hand.
Wait one minute and then use a rag to wipe off any excess oil.

<u>Wax is applied</u> in the same way, but without having to degrease before or wipe the chain after. It needs applying more often, and around 24 hours before riding to give it enough time to properly soak into the chain. It doesn't hold well in damp conditions, but it does mean the chain becomes less clogged up with dirt and is easier to clean. Main issue: You need a perfectly degreased chain, cassette, and chainring before applying it, otherwise it won't hold well.

CLEANING=LOVE

Taking a shower every day is common but likely unnecessary, while maintaining your everyday bike is necessary—and all too uncommon! *Naughty, naughty*

Not to turn it into a fetish, but keeping your bike as clean as possible helps prevent wear and tear, especially of the chain, cassette, chainrings, and the rims. Incidentally, it's best to keep your bike covered. A bit of rain or sun won't hurt it but regular exposure leads to accelerated deterioration.

<u>Cleaning with a damp cloth</u> (hot water + dish soap)—a good way to examine your bike in detail and reach hidden areas.

If you have a rim brake (≠ wheels with disc brakes)

To clean brake rotors: acetone or alcohol

And to scrub the sprockets: an old toothbrush

Hosing down a bike is effective, but avoid bearings (hubs, bottom bracket) and the chain

The more you regularly clean your bike, the less of a drag it is!

A tip from Scandinavia: Bestowing a little name on the items you cherish (my bike, for instance, is called Albatros) automatically gives them more sentimental value. You then look after them that much better and they last much longer!

DROPPED CHAIN

S**t! The chain isn't responding anymore—it's fallen from the cassette or the chainring or seems to be jammed... _Stop pedaling immediately_ to prevent serious damage.

Give some slack to the chain

If the chain is stuck in the crankset or is off the cassette, spend some time observing the problem before playing on its lateral flexibility—or even determinedly pulling on it—to get it out of trouble.

To get the chain back onto the crankset: with your left hand, push the bottom of the derailleur cage toward the crankset to give more slack on the chain and so enable you to manipulate it more easily.

The cause of a chain drop can be badly set-up derailleurs. If you don't address this, the chain will drop again. → p. 118

INFLATING/DEFLATING

Some pumps screw onto the valve, others clip on. Most fit two standard valve types:

• _Presta_ (ø 6 mm): Has a head that unscrews and that you press on to let out air. Tubeless valves have a core (top part of the valve) that can be unscrewed and changed if it's twisted or blocked.

• _Schrader_ (ø 8 mm): More robust, they're found on mountain bike tubes and have an inner pin that is pressed to let air out. Their diameter doesn't fit every rim, and they need a cap on them to avoid becoming clogged up.

Presta

Schrader

Tire pressure recommendations p. 38

TAKING OFF/PUTTING BACK ON A WHEEL

The first stage in repairing a puncture in the inner tube (see following page), changing a tire (p. 114), or putting your bike in a car or in a case to travel by train (p. 96).

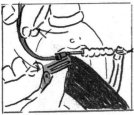 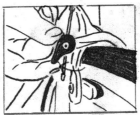 

V- or cantilever brake: Undo the cable.

Road brake: Loosen the cable using the little lever on the brake, or by pushing the small button on the brake lever.

① _Rim brake: Open the caliper_ to release its grip, which can prevent an inflated tire from sliding in or out between the brakes. _Hydraulic disc brake:_ Careful not to pull the brake lever once the wheel has been removed. If the pistons get pushed inward, they'll need to be readjusted. ☺ Placing a spacer between the brake pads avoids this inconvenience.

② Loosen the axle.
Some fork arms have small safety notches that hold the wheel on. In these cases, you'll need to loosen the axle a bit more.

③ Remove the wheel.
With the rear wheel, slacken the derailleurs (put the bike into the small sprocket/small chainring) and pull the derailleur back while pushing the wheel out.

④ Putting the wheel back on:
Do the same in reverse. Watch out!
☞ The wheel must be centered and well seated.
☞ Quick release levers most be closed.
☞ The brake must be put back properly!

It's *the* thing all cyclists dread!
Yet as any doctor will tell you: "It's fate: We're all going
to let out a last breath some day!"

→ Repair kit p. 61 and anatomy of the wheel p. 131

<u>Preamble</u>. As soon as one of your tires feels abnormally soft,
stop to check it. If it just seems a little underinflated,
pump it back up and see if it holds. If it is very soft, it
needs repairing.

At each point: Stay cool

<u>Intro</u>. Settle yourself in a nice spot, near a bench in the shade,
for instance. You can turn the bike upside down, but that can damage the
saddle and the road brake/gear levers. Otherwise, if resting the bike on
its side, be careful not to press the rear derailleur into the ground.

① <u>Take off the wheel</u> (see previous page) and, if it's not
already flat, entirely deflate it.

② <u>Using two tire levers, remove one side of the tire.</u>
Careful not to pull or pinch the inner tube! Slide one tire lever
between the rim and the tire edge (tire bead). Unclip the tire by
lifting the lever, and then wedge it in place against a spoke. Using
the second tire lever, repeat the process two or three spokes
down. Then slide the second lever away from the first, until the
entire side of the tire comes away.   No need to take off the
                                       other side of the tire.

PUNCTURE

WITH AN INNER TUBE

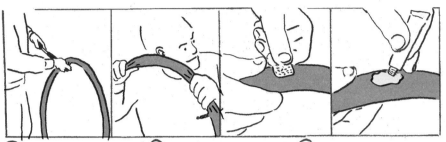

③ <u>Remove the inner tube.</u> Reinflate it and squeeze it to <u>find the hole.</u>

If the hole is so small that you neither hear nor feel anything, there is still the option to put the inner tube in a basin of water to find the leak—little air bubbles will spring from it.

④ Hole found! <u>Clean and then sand the area to be patched,</u> using sandpaper or a scraper: preparation for vulcanizing the rubber of the patch and the tire.

⑤ With the tube deflated, <u>apply vulcanization glue</u> (supplied with patches). The dose should be a little larger than the patch you plan to use. You'll then need to wait five minutes for it to dry.

> Of course, you can spare yourself steps 3, 4, 5, and 6 by fitting a new inner tube. ☺
> ☞ Its size must match that of the tire!

<u>Interval.</u> While the glue is drying, make sure that the source of the problem (thorn, broken glass, nail, shark's tooth) is no longer in place. <u>Inspect</u> the tire visually and by passing your hand along it. Shake it. Check the condition of the rim tape.

If you have the cruddy luck to find a hole in the tire, you can try a repair with a special patch or a piece of old tire and neoprene or patch glue—or even a food wrapper or dollar bill. You can also try to stitch it up with a fishing line. Alternatively, garbage can (sniff, sniff).

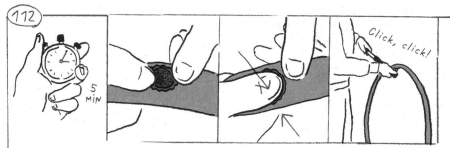

Click, click!

5 MIN

(6) It's dry! _Place the patch_ on the glued area and press down hard for a minute or so.

(7) _Put just a touch of air_ back into the inner tube to make it easier to put back into the tire.

Snap!

(8) _Replace the inner tube_ in the tire, starting with the valve—make sure it's nicely straight.

(9) _Put the edge of the tire_ back on starting on the side opposite to the valve so that you can do it entirely by hand.
If you start on the valve side, chances are you'll have no choice but to use a tire lever to finish getting the tire back on and in the process you risk pinching (and re-puncturing) the inner tube.

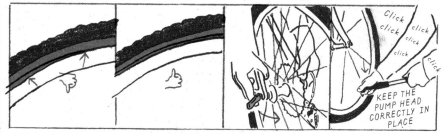

Click click click click click click

KEEP THE PUMP HEAD CORRECTLY IN PLACE

(10) _Partly reinflate_ the tire— enough to be confident that the tire edge (bead) is correctly in place.

Final act. Nothing left to do but put the wheel back on the bike, reassemble and check the brake (p. 36), and then inflate the tire in the proper manner (p. 38)!

TUBELESS PUNCTURE

→ Repair kit p. 61

Two main scenarios:

↘ The hole is quite small, but tubeless sealant can't do the job... The most likely reason for that is that we're out of liquid: FAIL! The remaining options are to reinflate the tire every mile, or to put on an inner tube—which will also be necessary in the event of a really big, bad hole.

→ The hole isn't huge, but tubeless sealant isn't managing to seal it up—it's a mess; it's spurting everywhere... So here we go with a plug. They're available in two different thicknesses, but generally we just go straight to the larger of the two.

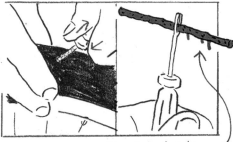

Coat the plug with patch glue to optimize the chances of a successful repair.

① _Clean the hole_ with a mini-file tool, taking care not to make the hole too much bigger or to damage the rim tape.

② _Place a plug_ into the tubeless plug insertion tool, flattening the center to allow it to pass through. No easy task.

③ Forcefully insert the plug into the hole

until there's only about 3 mm of it poking out from the tire. Then gently remove the tool, pinching the plug to make sure it stays inside the hole.

④ Reinflate and set off again.

The repair may not have totally sealed the hole, but the tubeless sealant should successfully take care of that as you ride.

If all goes well, the protruding part of the plug will be flattened and merge with the tire.

— # PUTTING ON A TIRE

Badly worn tread or studs, a big hole or un-fixable tear, cracked sidewalls...
A beat-up tire must be replaced to avoid repeated punctures and to stay safe. While replacing, check the state of the rim tape.

To remove a tire, see steps 1, 2, and 3 of "Repairing a puncture" (pp. 110–111).

To put on a tire, start with one side—paying attention to the direction in which the tire must roll, which is linked to the tread pattern on the edge of the tire (which removes water from it when cornering) or the studs. There is usually a small arrow marked on the side of the tire to help with this. Next install the inner tube and then put the second side of the tire onto the wheel (see steps 7, 8, 9, 10).

PUTTING ON A TUBELESS TIRE

Same method, except that rather than an inner tube we use a tubeless valve and—once the first side on the tire is on the wheel and after preparing the rim with special tubeless rim tape— we add a dose of tubeless sealant to the tire. Once both sides of the tire are on the wheel, you need to "pop" it so that it locks onto the rim and is fully sealed. A footpump works for certain tires; for others an air compressor or tubeless air canister is required. Make sure the beads are properly in place... The first inflation of the tire should be to the maximum pressure indicated on it. Then, to spread the sealant throughout the tire and create a solid seal, go for a little ride. It's then best to ride regularly on it to avoid the sealant drying in the tire.

Brake pads should be checked from to time. They need changing before there's any danger they damage the rim or disc or that they will no longer guarantee safe and effective braking. There are various standards linked to different types of brakes, with rubber or linings of varied durability and braking quality. So the trick will be to buy the right one!

Road brake pads   V-brake pads   Cantilever brake pads   Old-school brake pads

With cartridge brake pads, only the rubber has to be replaced. This is more environmentally friendly—and it's pretty neat that you avoid having to readjust the pad mounting each time you change it.

Disc brake pads

Disc braking involves applying a great power over a small surface area, when the pads have but a fine coating on them: They need replacing much more frequently than rim-brake pads.

They can also become "glazed," or be damaged by grease or lubricant = premature end. The discs wear out too—they need changing with every third new brake pad. Each of these changes needs to be bedded in. Have a look at an online tutorial.

How do you change a pad?
☞ Simply carefully remove the old one, and then follow the same procedure in reverse! 🔧
If in doubt, and if there are no instructions included with your new pad, look for the manual for your brake model.

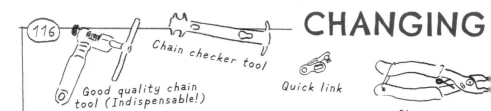

CHANGING

Chain checker tool

Good quality chain tool (Indispensable!)

Quick link

Pliers for quick link

CHECKING FOR WEAR AND TEAR

Over time, the chain's workload makes it stretch: Play is created at the rivets, causing the chain to lose rigidity. A stretched chain needs changing before it starts wearing on the sprockets and chainrings.

There are many factors that influence the lifespan of a chain—it can last for up to 5,000 miles on a road bike used for endurance-style riding, but less than 500 on a mountain bike that sees hard use.

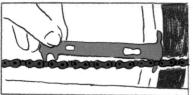

Measuring the wear between two parts of the chain using a dedicated tool. If both ends of the tool fit through the links…

Manual measuring: Put the chain on the big ring. Pinch the chain at 9 o'clock and use the other hand to pull one of the links positioned at 3 o'clock. If this link can be pulled away from the chainring…

→ The chain is finished! ←

OPENING A CHAIN

To open a quick link chain, you'll need a special pair of quick link removal pliers or to knot a strong piece of twine around a link to break it.

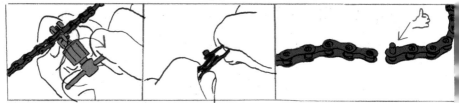

① Separate the chain: Place a link in the chain tool. Then turn the tool so that it pushes against the rivet (pin), keeping the rivet within the tool and stopping before it falls from the chain.

Leaving the rivet (pin) attached to the outer plate will make it possible to close the chain by pushing the rivet back in the opposite direction—no need to use a new pin or a quick link (see step 4).

A CHAIN

NEW CHAIN

BROKEN CHAIN

(2a) _Using a chain tool,_ shorten the chain so it has the same number of links as the previous one (see step 1). Compare the length of the old chain to that of the new one by lining them against one another on the ground or by counting the number of links. A new chain is generally too long, and the extra links within it can be useful for future repairs.

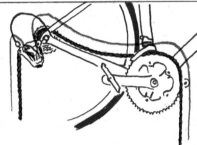

(2b) _Broken chain!_ Don't panic: It's fixable. Start by shortening it by removing the damaged links (see step 1). You can repair it without replacing the damaged links but the chain will then typically be too short to use the larger/largest sprockets— careful not to damage the rear derailleur!

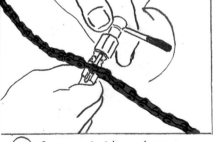

(3) _With the derailleurs in the position for the small sprocket and small chainring, put the chain in position._ Take care when passing the chain through the rear derailleur cage, doing so in the correct direction.

(4a) _Connect the chain_ using an internal and external link with either the original rivet pushed back in the opposite direction or a new rivet. If there is a stiff link after this is done, laterally twist the link in question to loosen it back up.

(4b) _Close the chain with a (new!) quick link—the easiest_ solution for reconnecting two internal links.

Hanging your bike
from a bike stand
= much easier adjustments!

ADJUSTING

*There are
still "friction,"
non-notched
gear shifters
out there—still
a great, low-
maintenance,
high-compatibil*
option.

The derailleurs guide the chain on the sprockets
and chainrings. The gear shifters control the chain
guide's "indexed" movements from one notch to another.*
The derailleurs' parallelogram mechanisms are used to
reposition the chain. → Drivetrain anatomy p. 132

Careful! The pedals must be turning at the point of changing gear, and not
have too much pressure applied to them. → p. 70

REAR DERAILLEUR
→ Derailleur anatomy p. 132

Four specific settings enable the chain to be
guided from the smallest to the largest sprocket
and vice versa, without "jumping" or falling off.
If the performance of the derailleur is gradually
worsening, it's probably that the cable is on
the fritz (see step 4) and/or that the derailleur
needs cleaning and oiling. If it's been subjected to
lateral stress (through a crash, for instance), its
hanger or cage plate could be twisted. You can
untwist them by forcing them just the right
amount, either by hand or using pliers.
Alternatively, replace them.

① B-screw (B-tension adjustment)
Adjusts the angle of the derailleur,
moving the upper pulley closer to or
farther away from the cassette. The
pulley must be about a quarter of an inch
away from the large sprocket when the
chain is in it. Tighten the screw to
increase the gap between the pulley
and the cassette; turn it the other
way to decrease it.

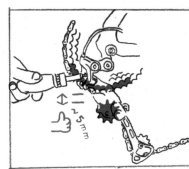

THE DERAILLEURS

② *The H-limit (high-speed)* screw determines the position of the derailleur when in the smallest cog—on the outside, when its pulleys have to be aligned with the small sprocket.

To set this position, the chain should be on the small sprocket and large chainring.

If the screw is set too tight: The chain won't be able to smoothly get down to the small sprocket. If it's set too loose: The chain risks getting wedged between the cassette and the derailleur hanger (eek!)

③ *The L-limit (low-speed)* screw determines the position of the derailleur when in the biggest cog—on the inside, when its pulleys must be aligned with the big sprocket.

To set this position, the chain should be on the big sprocket and small chainring.

If the screw is set too tight: The chain won't be able to get onto the big sprocket. If it's set too loose: The chain risks falling between the cassette and the spokes (ouch!).

You can adjust these screws before having even installed the derailleur cable and the chain.

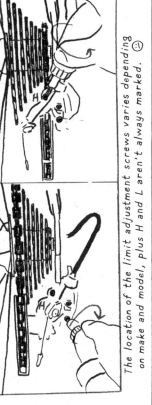

The location of the limit adjustment screws varies depending on make and model, plus H and L aren't always marked. ☺

→ ④ *The barrel adjuster* (on the gear shifter, frame, or derailleur) allows fine-tuning of the gear cable. Turn clockwise to loosen, counterclockwise to tighten.

If the derailleur has trouble moving the chain onto a larger sprocket when going up a notch on the gear lever: The cable needs tightening. Conversely, if the chain moves badly when going from the large sprocket to the smaller ones, you need to loosen it.

If adjustment via the barrel isn't sufficient, detach the cable and adjust its tension by hand.

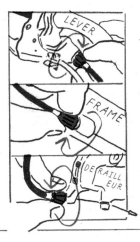

LEVER

FRAME

DERAILLEUR

FRONT DERAILLEUR

Same as the rear derailleur but in reverse:
In the lowest position, the chain guide is
toward the inside and guides the chain onto
the small chainring.
In the high position, the chain guide is
toward the outside to guide the chain
onto the big chainring.

Before touching the limit adjustment screws,
check the positioning of the derailleur:

- In the high position, the chain guide
  should be about 2 mm above the teeth on
  the big chainring.
- It should be well aligned with the chain
  connecting pins.

CORRECT ALIGNMENT

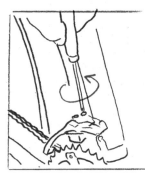

Adjust the L-limit
screw with the
chain positioned on
the small chainring
and big sprocket.

Adjust the H-limit
screw with the
chain positioned on
the big chainring
and small sprocket.

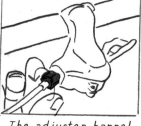

The adjuster barrel
tweaks cable tension.
Derailleur struggling
to move the chain
toward the big
chainring? Tighten up
the cable by unscrewing
the barrel (or vice
versa).

A worn chain or cassette, shabby cables or cable housing,
a twisted hanger or cage plate, a gear shifter that's broken
or done... So many possible reasons for settings to always be
imperfect, despite adjustment. ☹

A bike is made up of parts that are <u>subject to wear and tear.</u> With regular use, they will need changing after a while:

☞ Worn or dirty cables and housing lead to bad gear changes or to somewhat spongy braking. A cable can sometimes break, especially if it's frayed. Before threading a new cable into its housing, put a dab of oil on the end of it.

☞ Worn teeth on cassettes and chainrings make the chain wear out more quickly, stop gear indexing and cause chain jumps, make noise... The cassette is to be changed every two or three chains; the chainrings every three or four chains (for double or triple chainrings) or two chains (for single chainring), or sooner if the teeth are broken or the chainring bent.

☞ The bottom bracket and the headset need regular maintenance (cleaning/greasing), and changing after a while if they no longer move smoothly or if any cracks appear.

A creak or crack when you push hard on the pedals could come from the pedals themselves, from the freehub body, from a wheel axle, from poorly tensioned spokes, from loose chainring screws, from an aging carbon component...

With the right tools, perhaps supplemented by metal tubes to increase leverage, mechanical work on bikes doesn't require force.

For components attached by multiple screws, <u>tighten each screw incrementally</u> in turn. Move in a cross pattern if there are four.

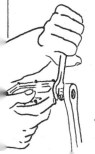

The left-hand pedal is marked with an "L." It has an <u>inverted thread</u> (clockwise to loosen, counter clockwise to tighten). On the right-hand pedal, it's the square taper bottom bracket cup which has the reverse thread. This means these parts don't come undone as you turn the pedals.

You can buy cycling tool kits that are more, less, or too comprehensive and doing so can prove economical—they're to be combined with a bike maintenance and repair manual. And don't forget penetrating oil, assembly grease, and grease that can be used on bearings!

Pay attention to the condition of your tools: A damaged screwdriver or Allen key can mess up your screw heads.

Allen key set
A good multi-tool will do the job, but a three-way Allen key is more practical and a torque wrench ideal for assembling with precision. Generally, avoid extreme force when tightening screws and bolts and use assembly grease.

Small flathead screwdriver

Small Phillips screwdriver

Tape measure
Boxcutter
Water pump pliers
(tongue and groove, or channellocks)
Roll of duct tape
Riveting or regular hammer

Cable cutters
For installing brake and gear cables and housing

15 mm wrench
For pedals

Set of flat wrenches
Or adjustable wrench (8 mm to 13 mm)

Good quality chain tool
Even if your multi-tool includes one
→ p. 118 for instructions

Quick link pliers
A link to simplified chain (dis)assembly

GEAR

A (VERY BRIEF) GUIDE TO WHICH TOOL DOES WHAT

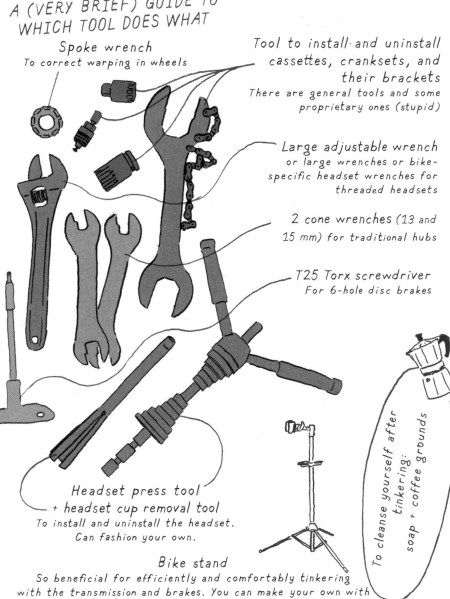

Spoke wrench
To correct warping in wheels

Tool to install and uninstall cassettes, cranksets, and their brackets
There are general tools and some proprietary ones (stupid)

Large adjustable wrench
or large wrenches or bike-specific headset wrenches for threaded headsets

2 cone wrenches (13 and 15 mm) for traditional hubs

T25 Torx screwdriver
For 6-hole disc brakes

Headset press tool + headset cup removal tool
To install and uninstall the headset. Can fashion your own.

Bike stand
So beneficial for efficiently and comfortably tinkering with the transmission and brakes. You can make your own with two straps attached to the ceiling.

To cleanse yourself after tinkering: soap + coffee grounds

COOPERATIVE BIKE SHOPS

There are quite a few and they're increasing in number, with a shared mindset of helping each cyclist toward self-sufficiency, saving them money, and helping them take care of the reliability of their equipment.

"If he's able to do it, why not you too?"
—Swanee, excerpt from the Dans la roue ("In the Wheel") podcast

The policies and atmospheres of these shops vary, linked to the people who bring these associations to life—my sincere thanks to those people! While there are still too many volunteers who won't let go of their tools and impose their "help"—some dudes, some not; some old, some not—inclusivity and friendliness is on the march with, among other things, women-only shops. The best approach is to knock on the door of a shop and meet the people there. These shops can also save our bacon when we're traveling.

The Bike Collectives Network (bikecollectives.org) brings together all community, cooperative, and collective shops in one searchable place. There were more than 250 of them in the US when this book went to print!

BIKE SHOPS ARE OUR FRIENDS

(Even if not all of them are very friendly)

Mechanic is a profession, with training, expertise, specialties, and a pro tool kit. Entrusting your bike to a professional mechanic is the price for peace of mind. They never skimp on advice, so there's the chance to come to them with your questions and to leave with new knowledge.

TUTORIALS

A load of tips and tricks can be learned online! But beware! It's fairly hard to work on a bike while also consulting a phone or computer without covering your device with grime!

• *Parktool.com/repair-help*
Professional tutorials from a pro tool brand.

Among the hodgepodge that is YouTube:
• *@PathLessPedaledTV* offers advice for non-competitive cyclists.
• *@Cade_Media* is more sporty but gives helpful tips.

"You can take lessons and learn everything there is to know about bike mechanics… but you can also decide that mechanics is only a tiny bit of cycling and that if you run into problems, you'll find solutions easily at hand around you."
—Louise Roussel, Le Guide du vélo au féminin
("The Women's Guide to Cycling")

THE COMPONENTS OF A BIKE

Finally, here's an illustrated glossary of the different parts that make up a bike (the majority are shown together in the picture on pages 4 and 5). Every component comes in different, rarely interchangeable, versions so all I have been able to outline here are the main types... A bike shop, an in-the-know acquaintance, or an internet forum can help you find the specific part you require, should the need arise.

A high price and newness aren't guarantees of reliability—in many cases, you'd be forgiven for thinking the opposite. Depending on the part, lightweight is often a synonym for fragile and uncomfortable and the hunt to save a gram of only relative interest, particularly for utility and touring bikes. Mid-range gear does the job well, and you can sometimes discover it available secondhand.

"A huge lightbulb moment: the day I grasped that a bike was not a WHOLE but a sum of pieces put together, that they were all of them removable and modifiable, and that you could even tweak them!"
—Julia Burtin-Zortea, journalist & writer

FRAME

Have I already said that a steel frame lasts much longer and is much more comfortable than an aluminum or carbon frame? Yes, sure, the latter two are lighter, stiffer, and there's no worries about corrosion. There's also titanium, for the wealthier among us. And bamboo or wood? Why not!

Eyelets for luggage rack and mudguard

There are various seat tube diameters. The most common is that to suit seatposts of ⌀27.2 mm diameter, then 24.4, 31.8...

Pivot screw bolts for V-brake or cantilever brake

Brackets to attach a disc brake

Head tube

Top tube

Seat tube

Seat stays

Down tube

Chain stays

Traditionally, the standard diameter for a head tube was 1 inch (25.4 mm). In the mid-'90s, the main standard became 1.125 inches (28.6 mm). In mountain and gravel biking, you now find conical head tubes (1.125 in at the top, 1.2 in at the bottom) and other such novelties. ☺

Derailleur hanger

Integrated into steel frames, or otherwise screwed on to act as a "fuse"—in the event of a crash, it is designed to break rather than the derailleur.

Pair of frame bolts for water bottle cages

Dropouts

Traditionally, for a quick-release wheel axle.

In recent years, mountain bike and gravel frames have been designed for a new, more rigid type of axle: the thru-axle.

Tube for bottom bracket

In most cases, "BSC" standard, also called "BSA" or "English." More exotic: Italian standard. Older: French standard.

Threaded headset (old-style headset)

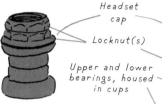

Headset cap

Locknut(s)

Upper and lower bearings, housed in cups

Upper and lower headset cups, sitting on either end of the head tube

Base plate/crown race, pushed into the base of the fork steering column

Threadless headset, with external cups

Headset tensioner top cap

+ star nut in fork steerer column

To tighten the stem on the fork

Semi-integrated headset for conical head tubes

☞ There is also a version that's integrated into the head tube.

The diameter of the head tube and the type of fork steerer column determine the choice of headset.

FORK

Three fork models among many others:

Road fork

Threaded head tube, for thread-ed headset and quill stem

Drilled to accommodate road-type brake

Steel legs + curved design = stability and absorption of small vibrations!

Classic dropouts for quick release wheel axle

Hybrid or gravel fork

Classic head tube

Pivot screw bolts for V-brake or cantilever brake

Eyelets for luggage rack and mudguard

Dropouts for IS (International Standard) or PM (Postmount)-type disc brake

Mountain bike suspension fork

Conical head tube

Varied amounts of suspension travel. The longer the travel is, the more shocks are absorbed— but also the more it increases the weight of the bike and the maintenance required.

Thru-axle

FRONT END

 Stem and handlebar choices → pp. 44–45

HANDLEBARS

UPRIGHT HANDLEBAR
Town bike type

QUILL STEM
Fixed into the fork steering column
thanks to its extender (plunger)

HANDLEBAR GRIP

RIGHT AND LEFT GEAR SHIFTERS
Controls the front and rear derailleurs

RIGHT BRAKE LEVER
Controls the rear brake

Traditionally, diameters of
25.4 mm (1.125 in) or 26 mm

LEFT BRAKE LEVER
Controls the front brake

THREADLESS STEM

ROAD HANDLEBAR

Screwed onto the fork steerer
column and firmly fixed there thanks
to a star nut → Headset p. 129

BRAKE LEVER/ GEAR SHIFTER

31.8 mm diameter

Brake hood

HANDLEBAR TAPE

Cap, or
possibly rear
view mirror
attached

Headset top
cover

Drops

Spacers
If the fork steerer column is long enough, spacers can
be placed below (maximum 5 cm) or above the stem to
adjust the riding position

Wheel and tire size → pp. 28–29
The right inflation and the right tires → p. 38
Fixing a puncture → p. 110

Tire width and profile are chosen based on riding style (→ p. 39) and its rim width

INNER TUBE

Tire bead

Valve

Tread

RIM

Rim tape
Protects the inner tube from drill holes and spoke nipples or, with a tubeless setup, seals the rim

Sidewall
Here you find information on the size of the tire, the direction in which it needs to rotate, advice on maximum and minimum pressures, etc.

Braking surface
On rims designed for pad brakes

Spoke nipple

Spoke
The spokes' balance of tension creates a perfectly circular wheel—without any kinks

Some details on tubeless tires p. 39 & 114

HUB

Threaded holes for disc brake

Bearings

Freehub body
With its ratchet mechanism, the cassette fixes onto it

There are also freewheels, which can be screwed on (to old wheels)

Inside you'll find all this mess

2 ↘

AXLE

Quick release
Available with a hexagonal, anti-theft, head

On fixies or old or budget bikes, the axle is locked with two nuts

Thru-axles are found on modern bikes, particularly mountain and gravel bikes. They can only be used with compatible hubs and frames!

DRIVE

Drivetrain principles → p. 10
Choose your drivetrain → p. 27
Adjust your derailleurs → p. 118

CHAIN
Chain care → p. 106

Link

CASSETTE
Made up of
the sprockets

REAR DERAILLEUR

Cable barrel
adjuster

B-screw

H-limit and
L-limit screws

Cage return spring
returns derailleur to
"relaxed"/"slack" position

Upper pulley and
bearings

Cage
made up of an inner
plate and an outer plate

Rivet
(pin)
Inner and outer links

End cap

DERAILLEUR
CABLE HOUSING

DERAILLEUR
CABLE

Body

Pulley spring

Lower pulley
With ball bearings

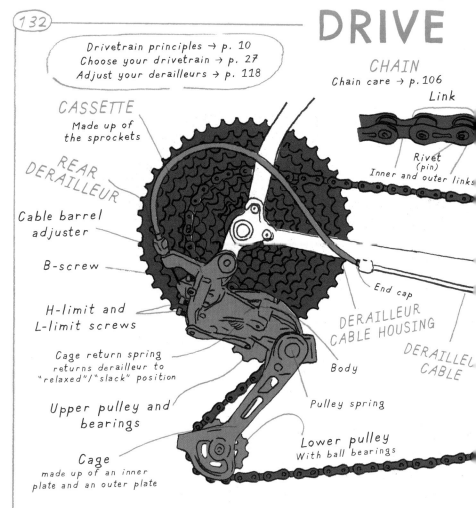

⚠ COMPATIBILITY OF COMPONENTS ⚠

The gear shifters are indexed for a precise number of sprockets
(from 3 to 13!) or chainrings (2 or 3). For simplicity's sake, they
are associated with derailleurs and cassettes from the same brand,
the number of gears and type of riding (road or mountain biking),
and with a chain designed for that number of gears (sprockets).

It would take a separate, regularly updated, book to detail the possible
combinations of transmission components. Best left to the geeks.

TRAIN

GEER SHIFTERS (Change gear → p. 70)

For upright handlebars

Trigger (thumb) shifter

Twist-grip shifters
You either love them or hate them.

Thumb shifters
Oldie but goodie, simple, durable, widely compatible.

For road handlebars

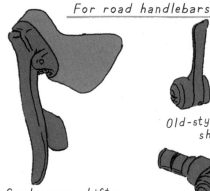

Old-style top tube shifters

Combo gear shifter and brake lever
Intuitive and pleasant to use. Operation varies slightly between brands.

Bar end shifter
Simple, reliable, and cost-effective. I love it!

ALTERNATIVE DRIVETRAINS

Internal hub gears

Valued by travelers, urban cyclists, or seaside cyclists who fear rust, all of whom appreciate a reliable system that needs little maintenance and that can't drop the chain.

Belt-drive

An alternative to the chain: cleaner, hardwearing, silent, and requiring almost no maintenance. Fits top-of-the-range bikes (notably urban ones) and requires a specific frame and drivetrain setup with an internal gear hub or gearbox. Replacement belt-drives are expensive and rarely found in stores.

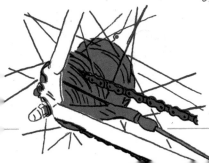

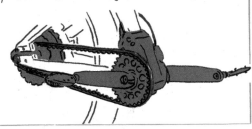

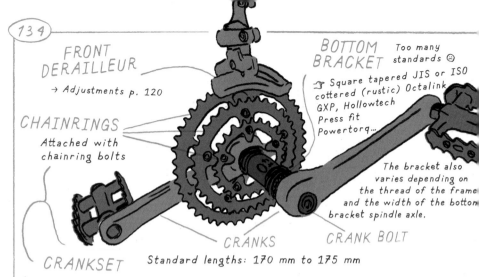

FRONT
DERAILLEUR
→ Adjustments p. 120

CHAINRINGS
Attached with
chainring bolts

BOTTOM
BRACKET   Too many
standards ☹

☞ Square tapered JIS or ISO
cottered (rustic) Octalink
GXP, Hollowtech
Press fit
Powertorq...

The bracket also
varies depending on
the thread of the frame
and the width of the bottom
bracket spindle axle.

CRANKS   CRANK BOLT
CRANKSET   Standard lengths: 170 mm to 175 mm

Setups vary in weight, stiffness, and crank length. There are also
diverse standards for chainring spacers and the types of associated
bottom bracket. You can change the chainrings, whether to offer
gearing that is better suited to you (→p. 27) or because they are worn.

Mountain bike triple crankset
Chainring: 44/34/22 teeth
Four bolts
Common sizes: 104/64 mm
↳ Also good for a single
chainring setup.

→ On modern cranksets, there
is also capacity for direct
mount chainrings.

→ Chainrings for the '90s
five-bolt mountain bike
cranksets with 94/58 mm
chainring sizes are much
harder to find!

Road triple crankset
Big chainring: 44 to 53 teeth
Small chainring: mini 24 teeth
Sizes: 135/, 130/, or 110/74 mm

Cottered crankset with single chainring—
a throwback found on old town bikes

"Compact" road crankset
Big chainring: 44 to 53 teeth
Small chainring: 33 to 44 teeth
Five bolts
Chainring size: 110 mm

→ In the traditional version of
this setup, the chainring size
is 130 mm (general standard)
or 135 mm (Campagnolo) and
the small chainring has a
minimum of 39 teeth—which is
pretty big for small. ☺

Perfectly satisfactory for day-to-day and leisure cycling—feet find their natural position on them, and most types of shoes work. With their large size and small bolts, mountain bike and BMX versions offer the best grip.

Clipless road pedals and shoes

Flat trekking pedal

Flat BMX/mountain bike pedal

Clipless mountain bike/gravel pedals and shoes

CLIPLESS PEDALS

Launched in the mid-'80s by Look and Bernard Tapie, special shoes clip into these pedals.

They give a bit of a boost to pedaling efficiency, by avoiding feet sliding on the pedals when the ground gets rough and by making it easier to lift the rear wheel to get over curb-like obstacles. And they offer a feeling of being completely at one with your bike (cooool!).

The attachment is made by a cleat fixed to the sole of the shoe, which must be carefully adjusted to avoid joint problems. Mountain bike versions are easy to walk in—the cleat is nestled in a depression in the sole and/or between two raised parts of the shoe tread; much more practical than road shoes. To unclip, you have to make a small outward twist of your heel. You can lose balance if you try to unclip too late, once you're already almost at a standstill… There's a knack to it. The first time you try you often end up falling. Toe clips are even dicier, for a slim performance gain.

Adjusting your brakes → p. 36
Braking → p. 72
Changing brake pads → p. 115

As with gear shifters, brake
levers for road or gravel
frames are incompatible
with upright handlebars—
and vice versa.

ROAD BIKE BRAKE LEVERS

BRAKE CABLE

For mountain
bike brake
levers

For road
bike brake
levers

For over 20
years now, gear
shifters and brake
levers have been combined
into one ergonomic
component. No need to
let go of the brakes to
change gear.

Two types of
brake cable
stops

Brake
hood. Can
be change
if it
becomes
worn.

Stainless steel versions last longer!

LEVERS FOR UPRIGHT HANDLEBARS

BRAKE CABLE HOUSING

If you're using cable brakes,
best to fit compressionless housing.

DISC BRAKE HOSE

Contains mineral oil brake fluid or DOT
fluid. Absolutely critical to use the
right liquid for the model you have.

Road brakes, cantilever, and road/touring mechanical (cable)
disc brakes have a shorter cable pull than V-brakes and mountain
bike mechanical disc brakes. In general, road-type levers are
short pull and mountain bike levers long pull.

Hydraulic disc brake gear is totally incompatible with
mechanical disc brake kit.

BRAKES

Any type of brake can be powerful—it depends on the quality and the condition of its components.* Frames and forks are generally only compatible with one type of brake (road, v-brake/ cantilever, or disc).

*In very damp conditions with a warped wheel, a disc brake is best. ☺

Barrel adjuster

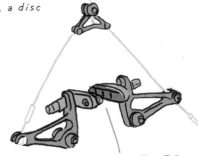

BRAKE PAD

ROAD BRAKE
Dual- or single-pivot

As with road frames, very limited in the width of tire they can accommodate. Some models allow you to run tires that are a little wider (maximum around 35 mm).

V-BRAKE/CANTILEVER

Prior to the arrival of disc brakes, these pivot-screw mounted brakes were on every mountain bike and hybrid. They're not great in mud or with a warped rim, but they're light, reliable, economical, and simple to maintain.

ROTOR

Fixed with Centerlock hub or with six screws.

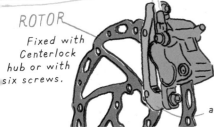

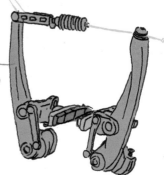

Brake adapter often required.

HYDRAULIC DISC BRAKE
Very powerful, very pleasant to the touch, it requires specific gear and fairly detailed maintenance.

Fitted on town bikes, <u>drum or coaster brake</u>s are part of the hub.
Nice: They require almost no maintenance.

SEAT

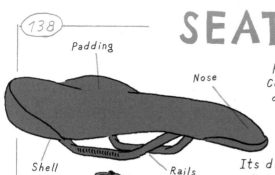

Padding

Nose

Shell

Rails

SADDLE

Pages 40–43 say it all!
Concerning "comfortable" saddle
covers—another marketing gimmick!
Better to find a saddle that fits.

Saddle clamp
On old models, it can be detached from the seatpost

Varied diameters—
selection must be made carefully (1 mm counts!) depending on the frame

Telescopic version available for mountain bikes, or with suspension for those who want extra comfort

SEATPOST

Its diameter is determined by what will fit snugly into the frame's seat tube.

It must sit deeply enough that it doesn't twist the end of the seatpost (damage that is irreparable!) —that means about an inch below where the seat stays meet the seatpost, or that at least a third of its length should be sitting within the seatpost.

There are shorter and longer seatposts, with more or less setback; you can change the seatpost according to your preferred saddle setup (p. 42).

Important mechanical tip: When putting an aluminum seatpost into a steel frame, apply a bit of grease first. This will stop the two becoming "welded" together over time.

SEATPOST CLAMP

A specific size will be required depending on the frame
→ see seat tube diameter.

Tighten well so that the seatpost doesn't move but so it's not too tight either, to avoid damaging the screw (and, if it's carbon, the seatpost). There are quick-release versions—not advised for use in towns, to avoid having the post and your saddle filched. Anti-theft versions certainly protect the seatpost but not the saddle, which can still be removed from the top of the post. ☺

BOTTLE CAGES

My worst experience when on a cycling trip? Summer 2013 on the Vélodyssée, the long-distance cycling route that runs along the west side of France, en route to Spain with Isabel. I'm riding right beside her on a brief descent—a harmless one, but the road is bumpy because of the roots of the surrounding pine trees. My bike shakes and one of my water bottles slides out of its cage... right into Isa's path! Impossible for her to avoid it, and she crashes. Result: a bad sprain, a month on crutches, a miserable time getting through the rest of the trip, and long-lasting post-fall trauma to deal with.

So a water bottle cage must firmly hold the bottle within it! And for off-road riding, the cage must be strong enough that it doesn't break over time and with all the shocks it receives. Mountain bike–specific models are the most robust.

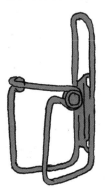

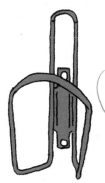

Certain frames (and forks) have capacity for additional bottle holders. You can use this for "cargo cages," which are handy for carrying water reserves, a bottle full of tools, a two-liter capacity waterproof bag...

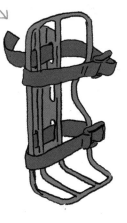

WATER BOTTLES

Using bike-specific water bottles is much safer than using regular bottles of mineral water.

A plastic water bottle cage will avoid scratches and noise when using bottles made from stainless steel or aluminum.

TO GO

> "The bike is the new witches' broomstick."
> —Ophélie Laffuge, excerpt from *Le Grew* podcast

COOPERATIVE BIKE SHOPS

To find cooperative bike shops near you: bikecollectives.org

THE LEAGUE OF AMERICAN BICYCLISTS

Follow and support the League to drive the development of the bike as a method of transport: bikeleague.org

VÉLORUTIONS & CRITICAL MASS

Live in a big town? Local cyclists will undoubtedly organize festivities, bike rides, and bike lessons. Meeting and riding with others is really motivating.

BOOKS

Just Ride: A Radically Practical Guide to Riding Your Bike, Grant Petersen (Workman Publishing Company, 2012), a collection of tips and experiences that sets aside the deviant behaviors of performance cycling and invites you to enjoy a meaningful cycling experience.

Two Wheels Good: The History and Mystery of the Bicycle, Jody Rosen (Crown, 2022), a cultural history of an engineering marvel that shows how biking became an essential way of life around the world.

Need for the Bike, Paul Fournel (Points, 2001), a lovely introduction to the sport of cycling from the quill of a passionate cyclist and sports writer.

How Cycling Can Save the World, Peter Walker (TarcherPerigee, 2017), a tour of cycling-friendly cities, the benefits to quality of life, and how we can take similar steps in our own communities.

Joy Ride: A Bike Odyssey from Alaska to Argentina (Kristen Jokinen, Hawthorne Books, 2023), the tale of an epic, 18,000-mile bicycle journey that shows how cycling brings people together.

FURTHER

PODCASTS

The Pedalshift Project, which helps listeners join the bike touring lifestyle to find more adventure and freedom

Bikes or Death, interviews about bikepacking and adventuring that highlights incredible cyclo-tourers

The War on Cars, on building less car-dependent communities

Joy Ride interviews amazing women who ride bikes

The Sprocket Podcast, conversations about bicycling, cyclo-touring, transit, and infrastructure

WEBSITES

SheldonBrown.com, as ugly as it is wonderful—a sort of bike bible

BikeForums.net—its name says it all

Bikepacking.com, where you go to dream about trips, read equipment tests, find guides on how to bikepack on your period, how to do without a chamois, how to ride with homemade bags, how to travel with a child or a dog...

PeopleForBikes.org and StreetsBlog.org, to encourage people to ride bikes and to support safe transit alternatives to cars

WarmShowers.org, international community dedicated to hosting cyclo-tourers for free

WorldBicycleRelief.org, "We are the world," as Lionel and Michael would sing

MOVIES

The documentary *The Breakaways* (Louise Roussel & Océane Le Pape, 2021) is a road bike movie "meeting those who ride, work and fight to open the way," while *Bikes vs Cars* (Fredrik Gertten, 2015), shows how much happier people are when they bike rather than drive, and how much more work there is to be done to design streets that keep them safe.

Always a pleasure to rewatch Jacques Tati as a bicycling mailman in *Jour de Fête* ("The Big Day") and the quiet cycling revolutionaries of screenwriter Gébé and director Jacques Doillon's *L'An 01* ("The Year 1"). The bike is also precious to the protagonist's quest for freedom in *Wadjda* by Haifaa al-Monsour.

November 2020, with Théo, Nico, and Victor on a Sunday trip in the Camargue area of France.

When you stop and want to prop up your bike but don't have a kickstand, avoid doing what is shown in this photo: The bikes are leaning on the wrong side, and if they fell it would be onto their rear derailleurs. ☺

ACKNOWLEDGMENTS

Enlightened and generous proofreading: Alizée De Pin, Judith Chouraqui, Clém Koren, Frédéric Paulet, Élisabeth Simonet, Didier Mazelier, Clémence Passot, Élise Sauvinet, Camille Dupouy, Sandra Trigano, Timothé Girard, Régis Behmo, Florence Voisin, Simon Taulelle, Grégoire Mazeaud. I adore you all.

Thanks to the team at Ulmer: Lila Hervé-Gruyer, Agathe Evrard, Guillaume Duprat, Raphaèle Dorniol, Antoine Isambert.

And thanks to the friends who responded to my little questionnaire!

For the North American edition, my thanks first to Claire Read. Translating my book required an extraordinary amount of care, patience, and skill; this edition wouldn't be possible, or as good, without her.

Thank you also to Nicholas Cizek and the rest of The Experiment team. Beth Bugler and Hannah Wood, thank you for your care and patience in keeping the layout looking so good.

Thanks also to everyone at Free Cycles in Missoula, Montana, for looking this over—especially Bob Giordano, who suggested some helpful additions.

The Experiment, LLC
220 East 23rd Street, Suite 600
New York, NY 10010-4658
theexperimentpublishing.com

This book is not intended as a substitute for the medical advice of physicians or other
clinicians. The authors and publisher expressly disclaim responsibility for any liability,
loss, or risk—personal or otherwise—which is incurred, directly or indirectly, as a
consequence of the use and application of any of the contents of this book.

THE EXPERIMENT and its colophon are registered trademarks of The Experiment, LLC.
Many of the designations used by manufacturers and sellers to distinguish their products
are claimed as trademarks. Where those designations appear in this book and The Experiment
was aware of a trademark claim, the designations have been capitalized. The Experiment's
books are available at special discounts when purchased in bulk for premiums and sales
promotions as well as for fundraising or educational use. For details, contact us at
info@theexperimentpublishing.com.

Library of Congress Cataloging-in-Publication Data available upon request

ISBN 978-1-891011-95-5
Ebook ISBN 978-1-891011-94-8

Cover and text design, illustrations, typography, and concept by Adrien Zammit
www.filloque-zammit.net — Instagram @zammitou + @zammouline
Translation by Claire Read

Manufactured in China

First printing June 2025
10 9 8 7 6 5 4 3 2 1

ABOUT THE AUTHOR

Like with so many kids, my first revolutions of the wheel are synonymous with joy. I like drawing just as much. And so I've never stopped doing either of them.

Flashback. The '90s, my high school years in Provence, and my buddy Arnaud and I are swept up by the mountain biking craze. We go up and down the hill behind our homes, get better at riding, and learn the basics of bicycle mechanics.

I take off for Lyon to study design. Five kilometers separate my dorm from school, and the Peugeot sports touring bike Grandpa Jean handed on to me is perfect for traveling between them while Lyon's shared bicycle hire scheme emerges. The rest of my studies take place in Paris, where I initially prefer public transportation until I treat myself to a touring bike with my first paycheck. I try out solo cycle-camping trips and get a taste for the delights and annoyances that go along with them. At the same time, I ride about 12 miles a day while commuting—my only regular exercise. At that time, the shared hire bikes and the fixie trend are coming in strong.

I continue my tour of French towns by living in Strasbourg for a year and for almost a decade in Marseilles, equipped with an "urbanized" mountain bike to deal with the nervy traffic and the other local pitfalls: tram rails, potholes, unruly pedestrians, cars failing to signal... I also acquire a third-hand road bike for jaunts locally or a little farther afield (as far as the Netherlands or Tuscany). I slip into a few Vélorutions movements and fall quickly for the spirit of gravel riding.

Well into my 30s—and having turned the page on Formes Vives, a graphic design collective created in 2008—I am beginning a new, more laidback chapter in my life and I settle in a little corner of the Auvergne that's populated by enthusiastic folk. I'm lacking very little in this "godforsaken hellhole" in the middle of the country, surrounded by gentle mountains. Like my friends Lambert, Ted, and Gaston, here too I do without a car and make most of my journeys by pedaling. Whether it's for socializing or work, I always take my bike along—also slipping more or less monthly cycling treks into my diary.

In 2025, I'm back in Marseille, with less free time again and a kid on the way! New bike adventures, ahoy!